Published by

The Key Consultancy Ltd
11 Kidderminster Road, Bromsgrove, Worcs. B61 7JJ

Tel: + 44 (0) 1527 575182
Fax: + 44 (0) 1527 576288

Website http://www.thekeyconsultancy.co.uk
E-mail: info@thekeyconsultancy.co.uk

D1390984

© The Key Consultancy Ltd 2004
Second edition
First published 1999

ISBN 0 9537272 0 3

Health and Safety Soundbites

A glossary of terms used in the discipline of occupational health and safety.

A word from the editor

The discipline of occupational health and safety is one of a very few which does not have a recognised and accredited vocabulary. It does however have a professional status which possesses a vast body of technical knowledge taught by universities and training organisations throughout the UK.

To many students embarking upon a career in occupational health and safety it means learning not one but several new languages. The language of the lawyer, the engineer, the medical practitioner, the psychologist and the occupational hygienist are all part of the Safety Practitioner's repertoire.

This glossary seeks to define and formalise a wide range of terms in one volume which will provide a quick and easy reference for those engaged in the profession. It contains definitions of almost all of the key words and concepts used in the NEBOSH* Diploma syllabus guide. It will prove a valuable resource for the student of occupational health and safety at any level, but will be equally at home in the reference library of any manager who has to communicate with Safety Practitioners* in their own language.

Thanks are due to my professional team of colleagues whose consensus has led to the interpretations of the terms contained in this book. References are given in alphabetical order as key words or phrases, supplementary references are given in bold type within the text.

John Gilbertson
M.Sc. Cert Ed. FIOSH. RSP

*Look it up

Contents

Disclaimer

Whilst every effort has been made to ensure the accuracy of the information contained in this book opinions may vary regarding some concepts.

The Key Consultancy Ltd accepts no responsibility for any loss arising from reliance on this content and readers should take steps to verify interpretations to their own satisfaction if there is doubt.

Absorbed Dose (radiation)	Quantity of energy imparted by **ionising radiation** to unit mass of matter such as tissue. Unit: **Gray**, symbol: Gy. 1 Gy = 1 joule per kilogram.
Absorption (noise)	The use of a material or structure to absorb noise energy and prevent its reflection.
Absorptive Silencers	Used to reduce noise from gas exhausts and gas jets by providing an absorbing medium at the exit of the jet. They attenuate more at higher frequencies.
Acceleration	Magnitude of vibration measured in ms^{-2} based upon an average acceleration level (Root Mean Square) measured by an **Accelerometer**.
Accelerometer	Instrument for measuring vibration that is weighted, or has a filter which reduces the sensitivity of the instrument to less damaging high and low frequency vibrations.
Acceptable Risk	A **risk** which is considered not to interfere with the normal conduct of life, provided that we are satisfied that reasonable precautions are in place. It is normally taken to be in the region of one in a million of a seriously adverse occurrence. See also **Unacceptable Risk** and **Tolerable Risk**.
Accident Costs	See **Direct Costs**, **Indirect Costs**, **Insured Costs** and **Uninsured Costs**.
Accident Rates	See **Frequency Rate**, **Incident Rate**, **Severity Rate** and **Mean Duration Rate**.
Accident Ratios	Triangular concepts introduced by **Heinrich** and **Bird** (among others) whose studies illustrated a relationship between major injuries, minor injuries and no-injury accidents.
Accident[1]	An unplanned event, arising out of an **unsafe act** or **unsafe condition**, which causes **injury** or **damage** or has the potential to do so. (The Key Consultancy Ltd)
Accident[2]	An undesired circumstance(s) which gives rise to ill health, **injury**, **damage**, production losses or increased liabilities. (**HSG65**). The term accident is now out of favour with the **HSE** who acknowledge its connotations with chance and misfortune which may lead some to adopt an attitude of inevitability in their treatment of these events. See **Incident**.

ACoP

Approved Code of Practice.

Acoustic Haven

An enclosure or cabin possessing noise attenuation characteristics where a worker can obtain relief from the need to constantly wear hearing protection devices.

Act of Parliament

Statutory code voted in by both Houses of Parliament which implements Government policy on social behaviour.

Activated Charcoal Tube

See **Adsorption Tube**.

Active Monitoring

Activity directed towards checking compliance with an organisation's OH&S management system.

Activity

Attribute of an amount of a **radionuclide**. It is used to describe the rate at which transformations occur in it. Unit: becquerel, symbol: Bq. 1 Bq = 1 transformation per second.

ACTS

Advisory Committee on Toxic Substances. An official committee which sets **occupational exposure limits** based upon assessments made by **WATCH** and taking into account, among other things: risks, evidence of health effects, socio-economic implications etc.

Actus Reus

An event or state of affairs which is forbidden by the **criminal law** - 'the guilty act', or (in **civil law**) the act which directly leads to a breach of the **duty of care**.

Acute Effects (health)

The immediate effect of a **chemical**, **biological** or **physical agent** after a single exposure.

Adsorption Tube

Atmospheric monitoring device comprising a small glass tube filled with charcoal adsorbent material. Air is drawn through the tube by means of a pump and any contaminant present is then adsorbed onto the charcoal. The charcoal is subsequently removed and analysed to determine the nature of contaminant and/or concentration.

Aerodynamic Diameter

The diameter of a hypothetical sphere of unit density (ie sg = 1.0) having the same terminal settling velocity as the particle in question, regardless of the particle's geometric size, shape and density.

Aerosol

A suspension of any solid particles or liquid droplets in air.

Agent of Change

See **Change Agent**.

AIDS	A syndrome caused by the human immunodeficiency virus which attacks the body's immune defence mechanism. The virus is transmitted via body fluids and workers most at risk include doctors, dentists and emergency services.
Air Cleaning Device	A component of a ventilation system which removes contaminants from outgoing or incoming air.
ALARA	As low as reasonably achievable - an expression used in risk reduction which defines a stricter standard than **ALARP** by requiring a test of technical feasibility and current knowledge to be taken into consideration.
ALARP	As low as reasonably practicable - an expression used in risk reduction to define a standard or point at which (the cost of) additional risk reduction measures would be grossly disproportionate to the benefits achieved.
Alienation	Condition experienced by an individual when their needs are not being fulfilled, leading to withdrawal or possible aggression.
Allergen	Any substance, usually a protein, which, taken into the body, makes the body hypersensitive (allergic) to it. See **allergy**.
Allergic Dermatitis	A condition of the skin occurring on subsequent exposure to a substance to which a person has become sensitised. Once sensitised, only a small dose is sufficient to cause a reaction.
Allergy	Special sensitivity to an allergen manifesting itself in asthma like symptoms, rashes, hayfever and eczema amongst other things.
Alpha Particle	A particle emitted by a **radionuclide** consisting of two **protons** plus two **neutrons**.
Alpha Radiation	A form of particulate **radiation** which causes ionisation. It is made up of swiftly moving nuclei of positively charged helium atoms. Because of their limited powers of penetration alpha particles present their main risk from contamination inside the body when alpha emitters are inhaled or ingested.
Alternating current (AC)	Electrical **current** which varies in direction and magnitude having the characteristics of a sine wave oscillation.

Alternative Means of Escape	An additional exit route provided where initial travel distance in a room exceeds the specified minimum.
Alveoli (plural)	The minute air sacs of the lungs where respiration occurs (Alveolus singular).
Alveolitis	Inflammation of the **alveoli** of the lungs caused by an allergic reaction. See **Extrinsic Allergic Alveolitis**.
Ames Test	A method for determining the carcinogenicity of substances based upon the belief that carcinogens induce gene mutation. Instead of animal testing, bacteria grown in a culture medium is used and mutant colonies observed and counted.
Ammonia	See Appendix 2 Commonly Occurring Substances.
Amosite	Brown **asbestos**.
Amplitude (noise)	The peak pressure level of a sound wave with respect to normal air pressure (i.e., maximum compression (+ve) or maximum rarefraction (-ve).
Anemometer	Instrument used for measurement of air speed. See **Hot Wire Anemometer** and **Rotating Vane Anemometer**.
Anthrax	A sometimes fatal zoonose which affects the skin or lung. It is transmitted through the inhalation of spores or contact with the skin. The bacteria which occurs primarily in animals can survive outside the host in the ground for many years. Occupations most at risk are those treating animal skins and hides.
Anthropology	A branch of the behavioural sciences concerned with the study of whole communities and societies seeking to illustrate interdependence and interrelatedness of social groups within them. Broadest study of mankind ie, mind, body, environment, race, evolution.
Anthropometry	The scientific measurement of the human body.
Antigen	A substance foreign to the body which causes the production of antibodies. See **Lymphocyte**.
APF	**Assigned Protection Factor.**
Aplastic Anaemia	The cessation of red corpuscle production in bone marrow caused by exposure to **benzene**, trinitrotoluene, irradiation and organic insecticides.

Appointed Person[1]	A person who is not a **first aider** but is appointed and trained by an employer to carry out duties involved in the management of a **first aid** emergency.
Appointed Person[2]	Arising out of **PUWER**, a person with suitable and sufficient training who is appointed in writing by an employer to inspect and test guards and/or protection devices on power presses.
Approved Code of Practice	A device introduced by s16 of the Health and Safety at Work etc Act 1974 by which the **Health and Safety Commission** may approve industrial standards and working practices which meet the requirements of a particular set of Regulations. ACoPs give advice on how to comply with the law and have special legal status in so far as they may be used in evidence to support a prosecution (or a defence) for breaches of Regulations.
Aptitude	The ability to deal with aspects of the environment. An innate ability to perform a particular behaviour.
Arc Eye	An extremely painful **conjunctivitis** including photophobia (unwillingness to look at light) follows a few hours after exposure to ultra-violet radiation used in welding. The condition usually involves the cornea as well as conjunctiva (keratoconjunctivitis).
Area Sampling	The collection of samples of airborne concentrations of **substances hazardous to health** by placing a sampling device at selected points in a workplace which may produce a representative sample of the contamination which exits.
Argyria	Silver-blue skin discolouration caused by long-term exposure to silver salts.
Argyris (Chris)	Management guru whose main relevance is his work into the effects of organisational control on the growth trends of a healthy **personality**.
Article 100a	See **Article 95**.
Article 118a	See **Article 137**.
Article 137	Article of the **Single European Act** aimed at harmonising the standards of safety of people at the workplace.
Article 95	Article of the **Single European Act** aimed at removing the barriers to trade for new machinery and equipment.

Asbestos	See Appendix 2 Commonly Occurring Substances.
Asbestosis	A **prescribed disease** which occurs predominantly in the deep lung producing fibrotic nodules which gradually conglomerate reducing lung function and causing breathing difficulties. Also notifiable under **RIDDOR** (see **Mesothelioma**).
Aspergillosis	A **prescribed disease** caused by exposure to the Aspergillus fungus commonly associated with asthma-like symptoms. It can occasionally grow in the eye or heart valves with serious consequences. Occupations at risk include farming and horticulture.
Asphyxiant	A substance which has the properties to suffocate a living being. See **Simple Asphyxiant** and **Chemical Asphyxiant**.
Assessed Risk	The level of risk (of a particular outcome) as valued by expert opinion and generally based upon relevant data, knowledge and experience, and probabilistic conclusions. See also **Estimated Risk**.
Assigned Protection Factor	The level of respiratory protection that can realistically be expected to be achieved in the workplace by 95% of adequately trained and supervised wearers using a properly functioning and correctly fitted **respiratory protective device**.
Assumed Protection Value (APV)	A prediction of the **noise** reduction possible to achieve in real use, usually calculated as the mean attenuation minus one standard deviation.
Asthma	See **Occupational Asthma**.
Atom	The smallest portion of an **element** that can combine chemically with other atoms.
Atomic Absorption Spectrometry	An analytical technique which involves the absorption of light energy by an atomic vapour. The wavelength at which absorption occurs is characteristic of the element; and the degree of absorption is a function of the concentration of atoms in the vapour.
Atomic Mass	The mass of an **isotope** of an **element** expressed in atomic mass units, which are defined as one-twelfth of the mass of an **atom** of carbon-12.
Atomic Number	The number of **protons** in the **nucleus** of an **atom** which determines its chemical properties.

Attention Mechanism   Component of human functioning which allows us to select particular information from the vast amount detectable by the senses.

Attenuation   The **noise** reduction achieved by control measures in **dB**.

Attenuation Data   Information provided by a supplier of hearing protection devices about the **attenuation** properties of their products.

Attitude   A predisposition to think, act or feel in a particular way about a particular issue.

Audiometry   A technique used for assessing the degree of hearing loss in a person.

Audit   See **Safety Audit**.

Authorised Person   A senior manager or authority in a company whose responsibility is to issue a **permit to work**. See also **Responsible Person**.

Authority   The ability to get things done because one's orders are seen to be legitimate or justified - **legitimate power**.

Autoignition Temperature   The lowest temperature at which a substance will ignite spontaneously (ie without the presence of a source of ignition).

Automatic Guard   A protective device linked to the action of a machine which moves the guard into position when the machine cycle begins, and in the process moves the operator away from the **danger zone**.

A-weighting   A mathematical weighting of the audible frequencies designed to mimic the response of the human ear to **noise**. It takes account of the fact that the ear is less sensitive to **noise** at very high or very low frequencies than it is at frequencies in the middle of the audible range

Back up System   A reliability engineering technique which activates a safety or protection device should the primary system fail, eg a mechanical-scotch.

Bacteria   Organisms which come in a variety of shapes eg spherical (cocci), rod shaped (bacilli) etc. They may exist as a single cell or grow in colonies many of them being able to survive independently of any other organism.

Ballistic Action
A **behaviour** which once initiated will continue to the end without conscious thought or external control, even if no longer appropriate in the circumstances.

Ballistic Over-learning
The over-learning of an activity to the point at which it can be delegated to a sub-controlling part of the brain.

Base Plate
A small flat metal plate fitted to the bottom end of a **scaffold standard** which increases the surface in contact with the ground.

Basic Cause
The element of failure or loss of control prior to the existence of the **immediate cause** of an **accident**. See **Root Causes**.

Basic Survey
A **sampling** approach which concentrates on assessing the 'worst case' and using this as an index of the overall risk. For large numbers of workers they should be divided into homogenous groups in relation to type of work, location, duration etc. The groups with the highest suspected exposure can then be studied ensuring that individual work patterns and exposure cycles have been adequately covered.

Bathtub Curve
Graphical representation of the expected failure rates of a component. So called because of its similarity to a bathtub.

BATNEEC
Best Available Technique Not Entailing Excessive Cost.

Becquerel
See **Activity**.

Behaviour
Description of what a person does in the context of others, action in response to a stimulus. An activity directly detectable by the senses of an observer.

Behaviour Modification
The systematic positive reinforcement of required **behaviour**, whilst at the same time ignoring or exercising negative reinforcement to eliminate unwanted **behaviour**.

Behavioural Science
A collective term used to describe those scientific disciplines which have varying degrees of concern with the study of human kind, see also **Psychology**, **Sociology**, **Anthropology** and **Ergonomics**.

Benchmark Guidance Value	A **biological monitoring** guidance value set at around the 90th percentile of available validated data. The data is obtained from those industries which employ good working practices. It is a level which can be achieved by the majority of industry by employing good working practices.
Bench-marking	A planned process by which an organisation compares its health and safety processes with other organisations with the objectives of reducing accidents and ill-health; improving legal compliance; and cutting compliance costs.
Benzene	See Appendix 2 Commonly Occurring Substances.
Best Available Technique Not Entailing Excessive Cost	An implied condition of authorisation to operate a process under **integrated pollution control** legislation.
Best Practicable Environmental Option	An underlying principle of **integrated pollution control** that consideration must be given to effects of emissions on all environmental media and that the least damaging route as a whole should be selected.
Best Practicable Means	A standard, usually indicated by a regulating authority, expressing views of what can be achieved in given circumstances. These are given in the form of published notes or documents.
Beta Particle	An **electron** emitted by the **nucleus** of a **radionuclide**. The electric charge may be positive, in which case the beta particle is called a **positron**.
Beta Radiation	A form of particulate **radiation** which causes ionisation. It involves electrons travelling at very high speed. Beta particles have moderate penetrating powers in soft tissue (about 1cm) causing superficial damage.
Beta-ray Absorption Instrument	A **direct reading instrument** for particulates which passes Beta particles from Carbon-14 source through dust collected on a plate. The absorption of **Beta radiation** is a function of the mass collected and a direct mass readout is given.
Biological Agent	Any **micro-organism**, cell structure, or human endoparasite (including any which have been genetically modified) which may cause infection, **allergy**, toxicity or otherwise create a risk to human health.

Biological Hazard	See **Biological Agent**.
Biological Monitoring	The measurement and assessment of hazardous substances or their metabolites in tissues, secretions, excreta or expired air, or any combination of these, in exposed workers. Measurements reflect absorption of a substance by all **routes of entry**. See **Benchmark Guidance Value** and **Health Guidance Value**.
Bird (Frank)	Guru of modern accident causation and prevention theory. Noted for his update of the **domino theory** and work on **accident ratios**.
Birdcage Scaffold	An independent **scaffold** constructed so as to provide its own support and structural integrity.
Boiling Liquid Expanding Vapour Explosion (BLEVE)	An **explosion** which normally results from the catastrophic failure of a pressure vessel containing liquefied flammable gases. The released **gas** ignites and a strongly radiating, rising fireball is created.
BPEO	**Best Practicable Environmental Option.**
Braces	The diagonal metal poles which connect the outer and inner standards of a **scaffold** giving support to the whole structure. Those running in line with the permanent structure are called cross braces, those running at right angles to it are called **ledger** braces.
Breach of Statutory Duty	A criminal offence - but one for which an injured person may make a civil claim if they have suffered injury as a result of the breach (unless specifically excluded in the statute itself).
Break Even Analysis	The analysis of the point in time when an investment will be repaid by the benefits estimated in a **cost benefit analysis**.
Breathing Apparatus	A **respiratory protective device** which provides air from an uncontaminated source which enables it to be used in oxygen deficient environments.
Breathing Zone	A notional hemisphere close to a person's nose and mouth in which the **sampling head** of a personal atmospheric monitoring device is positioned in order to provide a representative sample of exposure.
Brisance	The ability of an explosive substance to release energy at a rate which cannot be absorbed by the movement of an object and which causes shattering of objects in the path of the shock wave.

Brittle Failure	A fast fracture in a (generally) brittle material which occurs with little or no warning.
Brownian Motion	The movement in air of particles of less than 0.1 µm which behave like molecules and move randomly in air.
Brucellosis	A **zoonose** and **prescribed disease**, caused by contact with bacteria (brucella) in infected milk or discharges during animal birth. Transmission to humans is through broken skin or mucous membranes. Main occupations at risk are farmers, slaughterhouse workers and veterinary workers.
BS 8800:1996	Guide to Occupational Health and Safety Management Systems. Guidelines general principles of good safety management based upon two contemporary system approaches: **HSG65** and BS EN ISO 14001. See **OHSAS 18001**.
Buckling	A term used to describe the unstable compressive collapse of structural members eg scaffolding.
Bureaucracy	A style of organisation based upon legal-rational authority capable of producing a high degree of efficiency, characterised by a belief in rules and order and managed by distinct official roles. See **Role Culture**.
Burning-in	**De-bugging.**
Byssinosis	A form of **occupational asthma**, arising from exposure to inhaled cotton dust (among others) and causing permanent narrowing of the airways. It is a **prescribed disease** whose symptoms include progressive tightness in the chest, cough and shortness of breath.
Cancer	A lethal illness which can be brought on by exposure to **carcinogens**. Cancer can arise from very low exposures to relevant substances and may not manifest itself until some years after exposure. Called 'neoplastic' disease (a **neoplasm** is a new growth), cancer may take the form of a benign, local growing tumour, or a malignant fast growing, spreading tumour which can invade other parts of the body via the **lymphatic system** or blood stream.
Capacitance (electron)	The ability of a system to store electrical energy which is released back into the system in the opposite direction to the flow of current. See **Impedance**.

Capture Velocity	The air velocity required to capture an airborne contaminant at its point of origin and cause it to flow into an **LEV** hood.
Carbon Monoxide	A colourless, odourless **gas** whose presence in a room is undetectable to the occupants. See Appendix 2 Commonly Occurring Substances.
Carboxy haemoglobin	Haemoglobin which has been converted by exposure to **carbon monoxide** gas and turns the blood a bright crimson colour which indicates **carbon monoxide** poisoning by the cherry red appearance of the victim's face.
Carcinogen	A substance with a known propensity to cause **cancer**.
Case Law	Authoritative references of previous judicial decisions and interpretations which assist in the subsequent and consistent adjudication of cases. See **Judicial Precedent**.
Cataract	Lens opacities resulting from trauma (a penetrating wound or severe blow), heat (glassworker's eye) and irradiation (lasers and microwaves). Cataracts can be removed and replaced by artificial lenses or contact lenses.
CDM	Construction Design and Management Regulations.
CE Marking	A label or mark applied to a piece of equipment or a product to signify that it conforms to a specified **European Directive(s)**. (CE = Conformité Européen).
CEN	**Committee for European Normalisation.**
CENELEC	European Committee for Electro-technical Standardisation, see **CEN**.
Chain	Used for slings, the modern trend is for high tensile steel chains whose safe working load depends upon the material used in its manufacture and the diameter of the bar from which the chain is made.
Change Agent	The helper, person or group who is attempting to influence or effect change.
Chemical Agent	In the context of health and safety, a **chemical hazard** in the form of **dust**, **fume**, **mist**, **fibre**, **gas** or **vapour** which has the potential to cause harm.

Chemical Analogy

A method for determining the hazards of a chemical substance for which no empirical data is available. Such a substance may be presumed to have similar hazards and risks to other chemicals of similar composition or constitution.

Chemical Asphyxiant

A chemical substance which causes suffocation by diffusing across the lung/blood barrier and interfering with the respiration process. Examples are **carbon monoxide** which combines with haemoglobin in preference to oxygen and prevents further oxygen take up in the blood by forming **carboxy haemoglobin**; and hydrogen cyanide which interferes with enzyme reactions preventing cellular respiration. See also **Simple Asphyxiants**.

Chemical Hazard

See **Chemical Agent**.

CHIP

The Chemicals (Hazards, Information and Packaging for Supply) Regulations.

Chloracne

Unpleasant skin condition resulting from the effects of some polychlorinated aromatic hydrocarbons on sebaceous glands producing blackheads and cysts on the face and neck.

Chromatography

Chemical analysis technique used for separating or analysing a mixture of gases, liquids or dissolved substances. It is based upon the partition of two different and immiscible substances one of which is moving (the mobile phase) and one of which is stationary (the stationary phase).

Chrome Holes

See **Skin Ulceration**.

Chromium Compounds

See Appendix 2 Commonly Occurring Substances.

Chromium Mist

See **Chromium Compounds**.

Chromosomes

Rod-shaped bodies found in the **nucleus** of cells in the body. They contain the **genes**, or hereditary constituents. Human beings possess 23 pairs.

Chromic Acid Mist

See **Chromium Compounds**.

Chronic Effects (health)

The long term accumulated effect of a **chemical**, **biological**, or **physical agent** after prolonged or repeated exposure.

Chrysotile

White **asbestos**.

Cilia	Microscopic hairs on the lining cells covering mucous membranes. See **Mucociliary Escalator**.
Ciliary Escalator	See **Mucociliary Escalator**.
Circuit Load	The **current** flowing when an electrical circuit is operating normally on load.
Civil Law	A branch of law conferring rights on individuals and allowing redress against the wrong doer.
Civil Liability	Liability in **civil law** for harm or wrong done to an individual.
Claimant[1]	Term introduced by the **Woolf Report** (1999) to describe a person pursuing a claim under **civil law**. Replaces the word **plaintiff**.
Claimant[2]	A person claiming state benefit under the industrial injuries benefit scheme eg disability benefit for a **prescribed disease**.
Classical Conditioning	A **learning** process observed by Pavlov in which a naturally occurring **behaviour** could be elicited by simultaneously pairing the stimulus which produced it, with an artificial stimulus, eventually eliciting the same **behaviour** with the artificial stimulus alone.
Client	Under **CDM** is the person for whom work is carried out whether in-house or through **contractors**.
Closed System	A **system** which does not interact with its environment.
Coal Tar	See Appendix 2 Commonly Occurring Substances.
Code of Practice	**Approved Code of Practice.**
Coercive Power	The ability to influence the **behaviour** of people because they believe you are able and willing to administer penalties which they dislike. See also **Expert Power** and **Reward Power**.
Cold Stress	Hypothermia, a clinically diagnosed condition when the body core temperature drops below 35°C.
Collective Dose (radiation)	See **Collective Effective Dose**.
Collective Effective Dose	The quantity obtained by multiplying the average **effective dose** by the number of people exposed to a given source of **ionising radiation**. Unit: **man sievert**, symbol: man Sv.

Committee for European Normalisation	European Committee for Standardisation charged with responsibility for developing product standards across the **European Union**. (CEN stands for Comité Européen de Normalisation).
Common Law	A source of law which is not written in statute, but is developed over time by **judicial precedent**. Breaches of common law may lead to criminal offences (eg murder) or to civil torts (eg **negligence**).
Communication	One of the **four Cs** which involves the process of imparting knowledge or information. It is an essential part of an organisation which does not mean that every individual must be able to communicate with very other but each at least should be touched by the network of communication.
Compensation	A monetary award given to the victim of a civil wrong which varies according to the degree of harm done. See **Damages**.
Competence	One of the **four Cs** which involves the process of ensuring that the necessary skills and knowledge are available to carry out all tasks safely.
Competent Person[1]	A person with sufficient knowledge and experience to undertake a **noise** assessment. One who has the ability to work unsupervised and has a good understanding and practical experience of what information needs to be obtained, how to use and look after the instruments involved and how to present the information in an intelligible manner. (Noise at Work Regulations).
Competent Person[2]	One who has sufficient training and experience or knowledge and other qualities to be able to assist the employer in discharging the statutory duties imposed (**MHSW** Reg 6).
Competent Person[3]	Definitions are extended to include technical knowledge .... to prevent danger (**EAWR**), practical and theoretical knowledge and experience (**LOLER**).
Concept	A network of inferences that may be brought into play by an act of categorisation.

Conductor	Any material which is capable of conducting electricity (electricity is synonymous with electrical energy) and therefore includes both metals and all other conducting materials. The definition is not limited to conductors intended to carry **current** and so includes, for example, metal structures, salt water, ionised gases and conducting particles.
Confined Space	Any chamber, tank, vat, silo, pit, trench, pipe, sewer, flue, well or other similar space in which, by virtue of its enclosed nature there arises a reasonably foreseeable specified risk. These include loss of consciousness due to rise of body heat or asphyxiation, drowning due to rising liquid level or free flowing solid, serious injury arising from fire or explosion, or entrapment preventing escape: (Confined Space Regulations).
Confined Vapour Cloud Explosion	Explosion of a **vapour** cloud inside a container, room or building where the associated pressure rise is confined until rupture of the containment. See **UCVE**.
Conflagration	The progression of combustion to adjacent combustible materials not involved in the originating **deflagration**.
Conflict	Disagreement (which may be either functional or dysfunctional) leading to a power struggle.
Conjunctivitis	Painful eye condition characterised by redness, discomfort and watering of the eyes caused by irritant gases, like sulphur dioxide and ammonia can cause conjunctivitis. **Allergens** like plants and dyes sometimes produce a similar reaction.
Constructive Dismissal	A situation in which an employee terminates the **contract of employment** with or without notice because the conduct of the employer constitutes a repudiation of the **contract**. The employee accepts that repudiation by resigning.
Contract	An agreement made between two parties which is intended to be legally binding.
Contract of Employment	A binding agreement between an employer and employee containing explicit and implicit terms relating to the conditions of employment.
Contractor	A company or one of its employees not employed by an organisation but who is engaged under contract to work on the organisation's behalf. See also **Principal Contractor**.

Contributory Negligence	Consideration given to the behaviour of an injured person which determines a proportion of blame and causes the **damages** awarded to be reduced accordingly.
Control	One of the **four Cs** which involves the demonstration of commitment and leadership, supported by clear rules and procedures which are rigorously applied.
Control Interlocking	A safeguarding system for machinery in which the interlock switch is attached to the guard to detect movement, and open the switch contacts whenever the guard is not fully closed.
Control Measure	A technical, procedural or behavioural technique applied in specific circumstances to either eliminate risk or reduce it to an acceptable level.
Controlled Waste	Any waste from households or commercial or industrial premises. (Excludes agricultural and radioactive waste).
Co-operation	One of the **four Cs** which involves workers and their representatives in planning and reviewing performance, writing procedures and solving problems.
Coping Behaviour	Activity adopted by a person when satisfactions are threatened which may include eg. daydreaming, withdrawal, aggression, projection and regression (among others).
Corporate Killing	Proposed offence at the time of going to print intended to simplify bringing charges in the case of fatal accidents at work. It will be used in circumstances where the conduct of the company falls far below what can be reasonably expected in the circumstances.
Corporate Manslaughter	The concept that a company rather than an individual can be brought to justice for the death of an employee. Prosecutions to date have been fraught with difficulty because of the problems associated with proving **mens rea** (of a non-human defendant). See **Corporate Killing**.
Corrected Effective Temperature	'Corrected' to take into account radiation conditions by incorporating the black globe thermometer in place of the dry bulb.
Corrosive	The ability to cause severe damage to living tissue by chemical action.

CoSHH	Control of Substances Hazardous to Health Regulations.
Cost Benefit Analysis	A qualitative and quantitative assessment made of the data collected in relation to an initiative or change programme. To make a judgement we need to consider costs such as capital expenditure required, ongoing maintenance, training and likely payback term, and balance these against the benefits such as reduction in accident losses, improved attendance, better efficiency and higher production.
Council of Ministers	The supreme decision making body of the **European Union**. It comprises of the relevant ministers from each of the member states for the subject under discussion. Eg Minister of Agriculture, Trade and Industry etc.
County Court	Venue for the trial of civil cases of (usually) small value, presided over by a circuit judge.
Court of Appeal	Court composed of senior judges including the Lord Chancellor, the Lord Chief Justice, the Master of the Rolls and the Lords Justice of Appeal. Jurisdiction covers appeals from the **High Court**, **County Courts** and **Tribunals**.
Cranes and Lifting Machines	A variety of cranes and lifting machines can be found in use throughout the world's workplaces. They range from small beams with pulleys attached, through mobile cranes, to huge fixed gantries capable of lifting hundreds of tonnes. Small appliances are commonly called **hoists** but these should be distinguished from the legal meaning of the word. A more accurate description of small appliances would be a winch or block and tackle. See **Mobile Crane**, **Tower Crane** and **Overhead Travelling Crane**.
Creep	A permanent deformation in a material which occurs over a period of time, often associated with plant operating at high temperatures.
Crime	A specified breach of the criminal law (eg see section 33 of HASAWA for breaches) which requires proof by the prosecution of both **mens rea** and **actus reus**. Unless **strict liability** applies.
Criminal Law	Branch of law setting out societal standards for correct behaviour and conferring maximum penalties for non-compliance.

Crocidolite	Blue **asbestos**.
Cross Ventilation	Method of ventilating a building using the wind effect by opening and closing windows.
Crown Court	Trial venue for serious criminal offences presided over by a High Court Judge or a Circuit Judge and a jury. The court hears cases which are triable on indictment
Culture	See **Safety Culture**.
Current	The rate of flow of **electrons,** the unit of current is the ampere and is equal to the rate of flow 1 coulomb per second. See **Direct Current (DC)** and **Alternating Current (AC)**.
C-Weighting	A mathematical weighting applied to the audible frequencies often used for measurement of **peak-sound pressure level**.
Cyclone	**Air cleaning device** which uses a combination of centrifugal and gravitational forces to separate particles out of an air stream. Contaminated air is introduced tangentially so that solids are thrown outwards against the walls of the cyclone and fall to the bottom under gravity. Irrigated and multi versions exist.
Cyclone Head	**Sampling head** used to separate non-respirable dust from **respirable dust**. The **cyclone** system induces air to swirl upwards in the chamber and the lighter, **respirable dust** is collected on a **filter**.
Daily Personal Noise Exposure	See $L_{EP,d}$
Damage	**Loss** outcome of an **accident**.
Damage Control	A tool of **loss control** which involves the systematic reporting, investigation and control of those accidents which result in **damage** to property; with the objective of an overall reduction in the total number of accidents and subsequent costs to the company.
Damages	An award of **compensation** which is related to the amount of harm done. See **General Damages** and **Special Damages**.
Damping	The use of high mass/low stiffness materials applied to panels, screens, ducts, etc to reduce vibration in regions of resonance or coincidence.

Danger Zone	Any zone in or around machinery in which a person is exposed to a risk to health or safety from contact with a **dangerous part** of machinery or rotating stock bar.
Danger[1]	The inherent power of a thing to do harm, (an injurious consequence implicit in a **hazard**).
Danger[2]	Def: Electricity at Work Regulations 1989 "give rise to danger" - shock, burns, arcing, fire, explosion.
Dangerous Occurrence	A notifiable event (to the relevant **enforcement authority**) of a type specified in schedule 2 of **RIDDOR** which could have resulted in a reportable injury even if, in the circumstances, it did not do so, eg collapse of scaffold, failure of lifting equipment.
Dangerous Part (of machinery)	A reasonably foreseeable cause of injury to anybody acting in a way in which a human being may be reasonably expected to act in circumstances which may reasonably be expected to occur.
dB	**Decibel.**
dB(A)	Decibels (**A-weighting**).
dB(C)	Decibels (**C-weighting**).
Dead Man's Handle	Out of favour (and not politically correct) term for a **hold to operate** control.
De-bugging	Technique for determining the **reliability** of a component or system by testing under service conditions before assembly or production.
Decay	The process of spontaneous transformation of a **radionuclide**. The decrease in the **activity** of a **radioactive** substance.
Decay Product	A **nuclide** or **radionuclide** produced by **decay**. It may be formed directly from a **radionuclide** or as a result of a series of successive **decays** through several **radionuclides**.
Decibel	Unit of sound level used in noise exposure measurement.
Decision	This is the legislative vehicle by which individual Institutions of the **European Union** may implement various parts of the treaties for which they are responsible. They are generally of individual application and their requirements are binding in their entirety on the addressee.

Declaration of Conformity	A certificate drawn up by a **responsible person** which declares that the product complies with the relevant **essential health and safety requirements** of that particular product's **directive**.
Declaration of Incorporation	Where a machine, by definition, is intended to be incorporated into other machinery, the **responsible person** may draw up a declaration that no **CE marking** needs to be affixed until the whole machine is safe.
Defence Mechanism	**Coping Behaviours.**
Defendant	The accused person defending a claim under **civil law** or a prosecution under **criminal law**.
Deflagration	The rapid combustion of a substance or material.
Degreaser's Flush	Bright red flush of face and arms resulting from the combination of exposure to **Trichloroethylene** vapours and the consumption of alcohol.
Delegated Legislation	**Regulation.**
Department of Works and Pensions	At the time of writing, responsible for the Government's welfare reform agenda. Its aim is to promote opportunity and independence for all. It delivers support and advice through a modern network of services to people of working age, employers, pensioners, families and children and disabled people.
Dermatitis	An inflammatory condition of the skin caused by one or more external irritants. See **Primary Irritant** and **Secondary Irritant**.
Designating Order	A **statutory instrument** by which the Home Secretary may specify the types of premises which may be subject to the conditions of a **fire certificate**.
Designer	One who, under **CDM**, prepares drawings, design details, specifications and the bill of quantities in relation to the structure.
Detailed Survey	A highly sophisticated **sampling**[2] programme using rigorous sampling protocol and statistical analysis of results which concentrates accurate measurement of **TWA** exposures of 15 minutes and 8 hour duration and requires the entire period of a person's exposure to be covered by either one, or several consecutive samples. The process should be repeated on different days and on different shifts to cover the whole range of anticipated exposure conditions.

Detector Tube	See **Stain Tube Detector**.
Detonation	A **deflagration** with a coincident shock wave and **flame front** travelling through a flammable mixture at supersonic speed.
Dilution Ventilation	Any method by which air is encouraged to flow into and out of a workplace with the objective of reducing the background concentration of airborne contaminants. Such measures may include **cross-ventilation** and **stack effect** as well as the more conventional engineering methods. See also **Plenum Ventilation**.
Direct Current (DC)	**Current** flowing in one direction and having constant magnitude.
Direct Discrimination	Where on the grounds of sex, marital status or race a person is treated less favourably than a person of the opposite sex, a single person, or a person not of the same racial group would be treated.
Direct Reading Instrument	A self contained device used to measure the concentration of airborne contaminant which gives an instant readout of the level of contamination.
Directing Mind	Concept referred to by Lord Denning as far back as 1957 identifying senior managers as the brains behind corporate decision making. Their (managers') state of mind is the state of mind of the company.
Directive	See **European Directive**.
Direct Costs	Those costs associated with accidental losses which are directly attributable to the event and paid by the employer to the injured person in the form of medical expenses or insurance compensation payments. See also **Indirect Costs**, **Insured Costs** and **Uninsured Costs**.
Disability	A physical or mental impairment which has a substantial and long term adverse effect on a person's ability to carry out normal day to day activities (Disability Discrimination Act).
Disability Glare	Direct interference with vision from **glare** which is brighter than the area brightness in the visual field.

Disaster	A catastrophic event characterised by the fact that the casualties usually outweigh the facilities for treating them.
Disaster Plan	Contingency model for coping with and ameliorating the effects of a **disaster**.
Discomfort Glare	A condition which produces annoyance, irritability or distraction and is related to symptoms of visual fatigue such as inflammation and irritation of the eyes and lids, blurred or double vision and headaches, fatigue and giddiness. See **Disability Glare**.
Discrimination	The less favourable treatment of one individual over another because, of personal prejudices. See **Direct Discrimination** and **Indirect Discrimination**.
Dismissal	The termination of a contract of employment by the employer with or without notice. See **Summary Dismissal**, **Constructive Dismissal**, **Unfair Dismissal** and **Wrongful Dismissal**.
Displacement (vibration)	The amount of movement displayed by an object when a force is applied and released.
DNA	Deoxy-ribonucleic acid, the compound that controls the structure and function of cells and is the material of inheritance.
Domino Theory[1]	Accident causation model originally postulated by HW **Heinrich** which states that an injury at work is invariably the result of an accident which is the consequence of an unsafe act or condition generated by the fault of some person. Faults of person are in turn described as the result of genetic and social factors. If these are represented by 5 dominoes standing on end the 'inevitable' causal chain can be demonstrated. Modern approaches now tend to favour **multi causality theory** rather then the narrow causal path of the domino theory.
Domino Theory[2]	Heinrich's model was updated by Frank **Bird** who replaced the term unsafe acts and conditions with substandard acts and conditions. Faults of person was altered to job factors and personal factors and the initiating domino (genetic and social) was given the label 'management system failures'. **Bird** also added the attribute of chance to the result by adding categories of **damage** and **near miss** accidents at the result end. See **Multi Causality Theory**.

Dose	The product of the concentration of a **substance hazardous to health** and the duration of exposure to it.
Dose (radiation)	General term for quantity of **ionising radiation**. See **Absorbed Dose**, **Equivalent Dose**, **Effective Dose** and **Collective Effective Dose**.
Dosemeter	An instrument worn by a person during normal daily work routines which is designed to continuously measure noise exposure.
Dow Index	Procedure applied at design stage ranking fire, explosion and reaction hazards in chemical plant.
Dräger Tube	A proprietary make of **stain tube detector**.
Ductile Failure	A type of material failure which is almost exclusively due to a single overload in tension or compression. It is characterised by substantial plastic deformation at the point of fracture.
Dust	Small solid particles generated (usually) by mechanical attrition. See **Respirable Dust**, **Thoracic Dust** and **Total Inhalable Dust**.
Duty of Care[1]	**Common law** duty placed upon all persons to exercise reasonable care that their acts or omissions do not harm their neighbour. See **Neighbour Principle**.
Duty of Care[2]	Obligation placed upon the producer of waste and others under s34 of The Environmental Protection Act 'to take all such measures as are reasonable to prevent the escape of waste and to transfer it only to an authorised person' and 'to prevent a contravention of s33 and to provide sufficient information to enable the transferee to do likewise'.
DWP	**Department of Works and Pensions**
Ear Muff	**Ear protection** worn externally normally comprising a retaining band with two cups which enclose the outer ear.
Ear Plug	**Ear protection** in the form of a plug which is inserted into the entrance to the ear canal.

Ear Protection	Generic term used to cover all forms of hearing protection.
Ear Protection Zone	An area required to be demarcated with suitable signs in which a person is likely to be exposed to noise at or above the **second action level** or the **peak action level**.
Earth	A protective device by which an electrical circuit is connected to the general mass of earth so as to ensure an immediate discharge of energy reducing danger.
Earth Fault Loop Impedance	This is the **impedance** of the normal earth fault loop.
EAWR	The Electricity at Work Regulations.
E-coli	See **Eschericia coli**.
Education	Activity aimed at developing the knowledge, skills, moral values and understanding required to function effectively in a social environment (see **training**).
Effective Dose	The quantity obtained by multiplying the **equivalent dose** to various tissues and organs by a weighting factor appropriate to each and summing the products. Unit: **sievert**, symbol: Sv. Generally abbreviated to **dose**.
Effective Temperature Index	Originally intended for predicting comfort rather than **heat stress**, taking account of the wet bulb temperature, dry bulb temperature and air velocity.
EHO	Environmental Health Officer.
Electric Arc	**Ultraviolet radiation** generated by 'sparking' which can cause damage similar to severe sunburn and a painful eye condition known as 'arc-eye'. Molten metal particles from the arc itself can penetrate, burn and lodge in the flesh. These effects are additional to any radiated heat damage caused by the arc.
Electric Burn	Caused by the heating effect of the passage of electric **current** through body tissues, these occur in and on the skin layers at the point of contact with the electrical conductors which gave rise to the **electric shock**.
Electric Shock	Electric **current** may take multiple paths through the body causing muscular contractions, respiratory failure, fibrillation of the heart, cardiac arrest or injury from internal burns. Any of these can be fatal.

Electrical Equipment Every type of electrical equipment from for example a 400 KV overhead line to a battery-powered hand lamp, and also includes conductors used to distribute electrical energy such as cables, wires and leads and those used in the transmission at high voltage of bulk electrical energy, as in the national grid.

Electrical Explosion The violent and catastrophic rupture of any **electrical equipment** such as switchgear, motors and power cables which are liable to explode if they are subjected to excessive currents.

Electrical System All the constituent parts of a system, eg conductors and electrical equipment in it, this will include all of the electrical equipment connected together and the various electrical energy sources in that system.

Electrochemical Detector A **direct reading instrument** for inorganic gases in which a sensitive electrode, separated from the contaminant gas by a permeable membrane, is promoted into a chemical reaction with the electrolyte in which it is immersed. As the chemical reaction takes place a change in the electrical current in the electrochemical cell occurs which is proportional to the gas concentration.

Electromagnetic Field The region in which **electromagnetic radiation** from a source exerts an influence on another object with or without there being contact between them.

Electromagnetic Radiation Oscillating electric and magnetic fields travelling together through space. There are limitless possibilities to the range of frequencies which exist but the main types are listed in the form of a ranking as an **electromagnetic spectrum**.

Electromagnetic Spectrum A table of energy in which forms of **electromagnetic radiation** are ranked according to their wavelengths. eg Gamma rays, X-rays, ultra-violet, visible light, infrared, microwaves, and radio-waves. See **Ionising Radiation** and **Non-Ionising Radiation.**

Electron An elementary particle with low mass, 1/1836 that of a **proton**, and unit negative electric charge. Positively charged **electrons**, called **positrons**, also exist. See also **Beta Particle.**

Electron Capture Detector	In sample analysis, uses a radioactive source to ionise the carrier gas inside a chamber. This induces the gas to produce a steady stream of ions which can be measured as a steady current whose strength depends on the gas component and its concentration.
Electron Volt	Unit of energy employed in **radiation** physics. Equal to the energy gained by an **electron** in passing through a potential difference of 1 volt. Symbol: eV. 1 eV = 1.6 x 10^{-19} joule approximately.
Electrostatic Precipitator	An **air cleaning device** which utilises the principle of static attraction to remove **dust** particles from air. Capable of achieving very high degrees of efficiency, irrigated versions exist.
Element	A substance with **atoms** all of the same **atomic number**.
EMAS	Employment Medical Advisory Service.
Emergency Lighting	Battery (usually) powered lighting system which activates upon the failure of the mains electricity supply to illuminate escape or exit routes in occupied buildings.
Emergent Properties	Characteristics of a system which are tangible but cannot be attributed to any one component in particular, see **Synergy**.
EMF	See **Electromagnetic field**.
Employment Appeal Tribunal (EAT)	A tripartite body comprising **high court** judges nominated by the Lord Chancellor and a panel of lay members chosen from employers' and workers' organisations. Cases are heard by a judge and either two or four lay persons, all of whom have equal voting rights. Appeals against an **employment tribunal** decision can normally only be considered by the EAT if there has been an error of law.
Employment Tribunal	A tripartite body set up by statute to deal with certain minor matters determined by statute. It comprises a legally qualified chairperson and a representative from an employer's association and one from a worker's association or union.
Enclosure	A **control measure** involving the separation of a hazardous process from the external environment by keeping it under negative pressure for example.

Endocrine System	Comprises glands, like the pituitary, thyroid, pancreas, and the gonads, which control many functions from growth to glucose metabolism and reproduction.
Endotoxin	Intracellular toxin (retained within bacteria and liberated when bacteria disintegrates).
Enforcement Authority	An authority given powers by statute to enforce health, safety and environmental legislation. See **Health and Safety Executive (HSE)**, **Environmental Health Officer (EHO)** and **Environment Agency**.
Environment	All or any of the following media, namely, air, water and land; and one medium of air includes air within buildings and the air within other natural or man made structures above or below the ground (Environmental Protection Act).
Environment Agency	Regulatory body set up to administer environmental legislation in England and Wales. See **SEPA**.
Environmental Health Officer	An enforcement officer employed by local authorities having jurisdiction over spheres of non-industrial employment, (offices and shops etc). Powers are the same as **HSE** in occupational safety and health.
Epidemiology	The study of the distribution of disease and of the factors which determine it within a population.
Equivalent Continuous Sound Pressure Level	See L_{eq}.
Equivalent Dose (Radiation)	The quantity obtained by multiplying the **absorbed dose** by a factor to allow for the different effectiveness of the various **ionising radiations** in causing harm to tissue. Unit: **sievert**, symbol: Sv.
Ergonomics	Process by which work systems are designed so that machines, human tasks and the environment are compatible with the capabilities of the people using the system. Encompasses physical, physiological and psychological considerations.
Errors	A category of human failure which includes **skill-based errors** such as slips of action and lapses of memory, and mistakes such as **rule based mistakes** and **knowledge based mistakes**.
Erythema	Reddening of the skin caused by dilation of blood vessels.

Eschericia coli	Rod shaped bacterium commonly found in the large intestine of humans and other animals. Its presence in water is an indicator of faecal pollution and upon ingestion it can cause (severe) food poisoning.
Essential Health and Safety Requirements (EHSR)	A term used in some **European Directives** to describe certain safety features or standards to be incorporated in products placed on the European market (eg Annex I of the Machinery Directive).
Estimated Risk	The level of **risk** (of a particular outcome) where a degree of certainty or precision can be claimed. See **Risk Estimation**.
EU	**European Union.**
EUDS	Equivalent unit density sphere. See **Unit Density Sphere**.
European Agency for Safety and Health at Work	A tripartite **European Union** organisation which brings together representatives from three key decision-making groups in each of the EU's Member States - governments, employers and workers' organisations. The Agency acts as a catalyst for developing, collecting, analysing and disseminating information that improves the state of occupational safety and health in Europe.
European Commission	Civil service body which administers the programme of legislation emanating from **European Union**.
European Court of Justice	ECJ is a court of the **European Union**, independent of other community institutions, whose task is to interpret the European Constitution and other enactments in times of dispute. It can hear cases involving EU treaties and subordinate European legislation brought by, or against, the **Council of Ministers** or the **European Commission**. It can also provide preliminary rulings to national courts on the clarification of community law.
European Directive	A legal instrument of the **European Union** used frequently to harmonise the laws of member states. It is binding in principle (as regards the objective to be achieved) but leaves the choice of form and methods used to achieve it to the domestic legal processes of member states (see also **Decision**).
European Regulations	Legal acts which override the domestic legal systems of members states of the **European Union**. These apply directly in the form expressed and are binding in their entirety.

European Safety Agency   See **European Agency for Safety and Health at Work**.

European Union   A family of democratic European countries, committed to working together for peace and prosperity.

Event Tree Analysis   A technique used for assessing **major hazards** which starts at the initiating event and constructs a tree from that event through a number of paths representing the success or failure of each relevant control device. It is based upon a binary logic that the control will operate or fail to operate and a probability is assigned to each outcome. From this each failure path can be ranked to its relative importance.

Exceptional Violation   A **violation** created when something goes wrong and the operator believes that the only solution is to break the rules even though it could be seen as taking a risk. The benefits of following this course of action may appear to outweigh the risk. The accident at Chernobyl nuclear power station is a prime example of this type of behaviour, with engineers continuing to improvise after a mistake and making things worse. See **Routine Violation** and **Situational Violation**.

Excitation   A process by which **radiation** imparts energy to an **atom** or **molecule** without causing **ionisation**. It is dissipated as heat in tissue.

Excretion   The process of expelling toxic substances from the body through the kidneys via the urine, but also via bile (high molecular weight compounds), lungs (volatile hydrocarbons excreted unchanged), gastric juices (nicotine), breast milk (pesticides) and skin (iron).

Exotoxin   Toxin released from the exterior of an organism.

Expectation   A 'built in' model of the world outside our head which influences our behaviour in a given situation. If the world does not meet our expectation we compare reality with what we expect and modify our **behaviour** and future expectations accordingly. See **Stereotype**.

Expert Power   The ability to influence the **behaviour** of people because of superior knowledge and expertise relevant to the particular situation.

Explosion   The rapid release of energy arising from combustion processes, electrical systems or pressure storage systems. See also **Secondary Explosion**.

Explosion Power	The maximum over pressure which can be reached under the prevailing conditions, measured in bar or kNm^{-2}.
Explosion Violence	The rate at which the pressure of an explosion increases measured in bar/sec or $kNm^{-2}s$.
Explosive	A chemical substance or mixture in which fuel and **oxidising agent** are combined.
Exposure Limit	See **Occupational Exposure Limit**.
Express Term	A condition of a **contract of employment** that is expressly stated to form part of the contract and is subsequently binding.
Extra-high Pressure (electrical)	**Pressure** in a system (UK) normally exceeding 3000 volts where the electrical energy is used or supplied.
Extrinsic Allergic Alveolitis	Name given to a collection of diseases which cause allergic inflammation of the **alveoli**. It results from exposure to the spores of **fungi** found in mouldy hay and other vegetable matter. Common forms of the illness are Farmer's Lung, Bagassosis (mouldy sugar cane), Malt Worker's Lung and Mushroom Picker's Lung among others.
Eye bolt	A ring incorporating a threaded bolt which is connected to a **load** to create a lifting point.
Fabric Filter	**Air cleaning device** capable of high efficiency removal of dust contamination in air in same style as a vacuum cleaner.
Face Velocity	The velocity of air measured at the face of a local exhaust **capture hood**.
Factor of Safety	An allowance made during the design of a structure or appliance which seeks to ensure that applied stresses during use will be maintained well within the ultimate strength of the materials used. This allows for unexpected forces which may be encountered during use.
	$$\text{Factor of safety} = \frac{\text{Ultimate Strength}}{\text{Working Stress}}$$
Fail Active	Failure mode which will cause safety systems to activate in the event of general failure eg **emergency lighting** upon electricity supply failure.

Fail Generational	Failure mode in which the component failure does not prevent any essential service being performed.
Fail Passive	Failure mode in which the protection system operates and stops the process in the event of a failure in any of the systems components.
Fail to Danger	Failure mode where the protection system becomes inoperative if there is a failure in any of its components. In the event of a hazardous condition arising the process/plant will continue to operate without being tripped.
Fail to Safety	See **Fail Active**, **Fail Passive** and **Fail Generational**.
Failure Mode and Effects Analysis (FMEA)	An inductive analysis used to examine each component of a system to determine how various modes of failure might effect the system or any of its components.
Failure Tracing Method	An analytical technique of either inductive or deductive approach which makes a detailed assessment of a system and determines the methods and consequences of failure. See **Fault Tree Analysis (FTA)**, **Failure Mode and Effects Analysis (FMEA)**, **Hazard and Operability Study (HAZOP)** and **Event Tree Analysis (ETA)**.
Farmer's Lung	See **Aspergillosis**.
Fast Neutrons	**Neutrons** with energies in excess of 0.1 MeV and a corresponding velocity of about 4×10^6 m s^{-1}
Fatigue Failure	A mode of failure characterised by the slow growth of cracks in a material subjected to fluctuating stresses.
Fault Tree Analysis (FTA)	A failure oriented graphical technique providing a systematic description of the combination of possible occurrences which can lead to the specified failure or undesired event under investigation. Uses a top down flow chart to link elements via 'and/or' logic gates. Can be quantified using probability data.
Fibre	Small solid particle which has an aspect ratio of at least 3:1 with aerodynamic properties to penetrate deep into the lungs (eg asbestos).
Fibre Ropes	Used for slings, fibre ropes can be made from several materials eg: manila, hemp, sisal, coir and cotton.

Filter[1]	Term used to describe the human being's **attention mechanism**, a vast store of experiential information which can be accessed when required.
Filter[2]	An **air cleaning device** used in ventilation systems.
Filter[3]	Dust collection device used mainly for **personal sampling**. The three main filter materials in use are: Glass fibre, Membrane ('plastic') and Silver.
Final Exit	The termination of a fire escape route from a building giving direct access to a place of safety such as a street, passage or walkway sited to ensure that people can disperse safely.
Fire Alarm	Device used to warn occupants of a building of the outbreak of fire.
Fire Certificate	A compulsory document issued by the fire authority (unless exemptions apply) which requires the occupier of premises to satisfy certain fire safety conditions which may be specified.
Fire Door	A self closing fire resisting door which provides **stability**, **integrity** and **insulation** for a specified period of time, typically 30 or 60 minutes.
Fire Extinguisher	An appliance (usually portable) containing an extinguishing medium that can be expelled by the action of internal pressure and be directed onto a fire. The pressure may be stored pressure or created by a mixture of chemicals within the body of the extinguisher.
Fire Point	The lowest temperature at which the heat from combustion of a burning vapour is capable of producing sufficient vapour to maintain combustion.
Fire Resistance	See **Stability**, **Integrity** and **Insulation**.
Fire Stopping	The practice of stopping up openings with fire resisting filler in floors or ceiling where cables pipes or other services have passed through, in order to prevent the spread of fire or smoke.
First Action Level	The point at which the employer must carry out noise assessments of the exposure of the workforce. A **daily personal noise exposure** of 85dB(A) (at time of going to print).[1] See **Second Action Level** and **Peak Action level**.

[1] The forthcoming updated Noise at Work Regulations is likely to reduce the FAL to 80dB(A) $L_{EP,d}$

First Aid	Treatment for the purpose of preserving life and minimising the consequences of injury and illness until the help of a medical practitioner is obtained. Definition in the Health and Safety (First Aid) Regulations also includes the treatment of minor injuries which would otherwise receive no treatment or which do not need treatment by a medical practitioner.
First Aider	A person designated by the employer and trained on a course approved by the **HSE** (see **Appointed Person**).
Fixed Guard	A protective device, characterised by a permanent fixing device which cannot be displaced in a casual way, which either encloses the **dangerous part** (of machinery) or keeps the operator at a safe distance.
Flame Arrestor	A device fitted to the opening of an enclosure or connecting pipework whose function is to allow flow out, but prevent flames from being transmitted backwards.
Flame Front	The leading edge of a flame in a combustion reaction.
Flame Ionisation Detector	In sample analysis, uses a Hydrogen/Air (or Hydrogen/Oxygen) flame which ionises most organic compounds in the sample. The collection of **ions** by an electrode results in electrical **potential** which causes a flow of **current**. The size of the **current** is dependant on the nature of the substance and its concentration.
Flammable Gas Detector	A **direct reading instrument** for gases which operates on a simple electrical principle utilising a wheatstone bridge. A sample from the atmosphere is drawn through the instrument passing over a heated catalyst. Combustion occurs in the presence of flammable gas and the rise in temperature is accompanied by a corresponding rise in **resistance** which is proportional to the concentration of **gas** in the atmosphere.
Flare Stack	A system used to discharge and burn unwanted or excess flammable gas in a safe and controlled manner.
Flash Point	The lowest temperature at which there is sufficient vaporisation of a substance to produce a flash momentarily when a flame is applied.

FMA	See **FMEA**.
Fml^{-1}	Fibres per millilitre (of air), a numerical measure for dusts and other particulate matter.
Formal Group	A group created by an organisation to achieve specific objectives laid down in the organisation's goals.
Formal Organisation	See **Formal Structure**.
Formal Structure	(of an organisation). The official description of the hierarchy and departmentalisation within the organisation usually illustrated by means of an organisation chart. The pattern of human relations as defined by the systems, rules, policies and regulations of the company.
Four Cs	The elements of **competence**, **communication**, **control**, and **co-operation** said to play a great part in the development of **safety culture**.
Fractional Dead Time - (FDT)	The moment of time that a protection system is inactive and will therefore fail to operate on demand.
Fractional Noise Exposure	Personal noise exposure related to part of the working day or an activity.
Fracture Mechanics	A mathematical technique used to determine the failure of structural components by assessing the significance of defects in terms of their likelihood to promote brittle failure and metal fatigue.
Frame of Reference	A viewpoint which influences a person's approach to conflict. See **Unitary**, **Pluralist** and **Radical**.
Free Radical	A grouping of **atoms** that normally exists in combination with other **atoms** but can sometimes exist independently. They are generally very reactive in a chemical sense.
Frequency	The number of complete cycles of an electromagnetic wave in a second. Unit: Hertz, symbol: Hz. 1 Hz = 1 cycle per second.
Frequency (noise)	The number of pressure variations per second measured in units of Hertz (Hz).

Frequency Analysis Measurement and analysis of sound in its frequency components.

Frequency Rate (FR) Statistic used to illustrate the number of accidents (of a specified type) per 100,000 hours (or other constant*).

$$FR = \frac{\text{Total number of accidents}}{\text{Total person hours worked}} \times 100,000$$

*Note that the multiplier may vary for different organisations, agencies and countries. Use caution when making comparisons.

Fume Solid particles formed by the condensation of vaporised materials such as metals (eg welding fume). Usually submicron in diameter and very reactive.

Fume Cupboard A form of partial containment held at negative pressure by mechanical ventilation comprising an enclosed chamber accessible via a sliding/sash door. Used mainly for materials possessing toxic, corrosive or flammable characteristics.

Fungi Spore forming organisms which grow as budding cells or through the formation of filaments.

Fuse A protective device designed to cut off the electrical supply to a circuit when the **current** flow exceeds a predetermined value.

Gamma Radiation A form of **ionising radiation** emitted by the nucleus of an **atom** as pure energy and travelling at the speed of light. Gamma radiation has great penetrating powers and can interact with the matter through which it is passing.

Gamma Ray A discrete quantity of electromagnetic energy without mass or charge emitted by a **radionuclide**.

Gas Elements or compounds of low molecular weight which exist purely in the gaseous phase under normal conditions.

Gas Liquid Chromatography The mobile phase consists of a gas such as helium, nitrogen, hydrogen or argon at pressures of 10 - 50 psi. The stationary phase consists of a packed column or a capillary column which is a small open tube. Each is impregnated or coated with a liquid chosen on its polarity and that of the substances to be separated.

Geiger-Müller Tube	A glass or metal envelope containing a **gas** at low pressure and two electrodes which measure the discharges of **Ionising radiation** by registering them as electric pulses in a counter. The number of pulses is related to **dose**.
General Damages	**Compensation** awarded where no exact sum is calculable, ie for pain and suffering, loss of amenity, future income, social isolation and loss of (marriage/employment) prospects. These can be further broken down into **pecuniary damages** and **non-pecuniary damages**.
Generic Risk Assessment	A general **risk assessment** of a 'type' or particular circumstances which are considered to be representative of similar risks wherever they are encountered.
Genes	The biological units of heredity. They are arranged along the length of **chromosomes**.
Genotoxic	A chemical that damages chromosomal structures.
Glanders	A **prescribed disease** of the **zoonose** variety which is hosted by horses, donkeys, mules and camels. It is rare in the UK, transmitted to humans via infected animal feed and water. Occupations at risk include animal workers and laboratory technicians.
Glare	See **Disability Glare** and **Discomfort Glare**.
Goal Setting Legislation	Acts and regulations whose objectives are to require the duty holders to establish controls that are relevant to their operating circumstances rather than prescribe wide ranging, all-encompassing requirements.
Grab Sample	Monitoring technique for airborne containments which gives a 'point of time' measure of the level of contamination at a selected place.
Gravimetric	Term used to express concentrations (by weight/volume) of all materials in measures of milligrams of substances per cubic metre of air (mgm^{-3}).
Gray	See **Absorbed Dose**.
Green Paper	A statement of the Government's intention to pursue a course of action, used in consultation processes to gauge public opinion.

Group	A number of people cooperating in the pursuit of common goals see **Formal Group**, **Informal Group**, **Primary Group**, **Secondary Group**, **Peer Group and Reference Group**.
Guard Rail	A protective rail fixed to a working platform whose purpose is to prevent persons falling.
Guidance Notes	Official series of publications issued by the **Health and Safety Executive** which illustrate best practice for a variety of occupational issues.
Habituation	The gradual acclimatisation or familiarisation with a phenomenon or set of circumstances to the point at which it goes unnoticed.
Half-life	The time taken for the **activity** of a **radionuclide** to lose half of its value by **decay**.
Halo Effect	The influencing effect of appearance or conditions on a person's judgement such as dress, speech, cleanliness, tidiness. Halo can be positive or negative and is reinforced by **stereotypes**.
Hand Arm Vibration Syndrome	Collective description for injuries to workers whose hands are regularly exposed to high vibration, such as "dead finger", "dead hand", and "**vibration white finger**" (VWF).
Handy (Charles)	Management guru of more recent times noted for witty and perceptive analysis of organisational behaviours (read his books). See **Role Culture**.
Hard System	A **system** comprised of mainly inanimate things with well structured components and definable attributes not dependant upon interpretation by an observer.
Harmful	A designation given to a substance which presents a risk of ill-health.
HASAWA	**The Health and Safety at Work etc Act 1974.**
HAVS	**Hand Arm Vibration Syndrome**
Hazard Analysis	A systematic exploration and recording of the propensity for injury in the hazards associated with an activity.

Hazard and Operability Study (HAZOP)	A formal systematic method for the critical examination of a process in order to assess the hazard potential of the malfunction or maloperation of individual components and their effect on the system as a whole. Carried out at design stage and subsequently as plant is commissioned or modified.
Hazard Indexing	A technique pioneered by the chemical industries which ranks hazards and their severity. Eg **Dow Index** and **Mond Index**.
Hazard[1]	An exposed **danger**, a condition or practice (**behaviour**) which has the potential to do harm. See **Major Hazard**.
Hazard[2]	The potential to cause harm, **damage**, production losses or increased liability (**HSG65**).
Health and Safety Commission	A tripartite body set up under the provisions of section 10 of the Health and Safety at Work etc Act 1974. It comprises a chairperson appointed by the Secretary of State and between six and nine members as follows: three from employer organisations, three from employee organisations and three from Local Authorities and other such bodies. It has the function of formulating policy.
Health and Safety Executive	A body appointed by the **HSC** to implement policy. It is an **enforcement authority** possessing regulatory powers in the field of occupational safety and health. Jurisdiction of its inspectors is mainly in the industrial and high risk sectors of employment but includes educational establishments, fairgrounds and domestic gas.
Health and Safety File	Under **CDM** a file containing design information relating to health and safety and information which may be needed by anyone carrying out construction or cleaning work on the structure.
Health and Safety Plan	A pre-construction plan prepared by the **client** and **planning supervisor** which includes a description of the project, proposed timings of the project, details of risks to persons during the project, information that any **contractor** may need to enable demonstrations of competence and information which contractors will need to comply with their duties.
Health Guidance Value	A biological monitoring guidance value set at a level at which there is no indication from the scientific evidence available that the substance is likely to be injurious to health. It is set where a clear relationship can be established between biological concentrations and health effects.

Health Surveillance	Aspect of worker monitoring when exposed to specified substances under **CoSHH** with the objective of detecting adverse changes in health at as early a stage as possible and to assist in evaluating the effectiveness of control measures. Requirements for health surveillance also exist in the Management of Health and Safety at Work Regulations. See also **Medical Surveillance**.
Hearing Protection	See **Ear Protection**.
Heat Stress	A consequence of the body's thermoregulatory system breaking down resulting in a rapid increase in the core temperature to 41°C or above.
Heat Stress Indices	Tables which combine the environmental variables into a single value which quantitatively describes the amount of stress that a thermal environment places on an individual.
Heinrich (Herbert W)	Said to be the father of occupational safety and health, original author of 'Industrial Accident Prevention' published in 1931. Early proponent of the **'iceberg' theory** for accident costs and the **domino theory** of accident causation.
Helminth	A worm like **parasite** which can enter the human host through contaminated or abraded skin. The only relevant **prescribed disease** in the UK is Ankylostomiasis which is caused by the nematode worm.
HEPA	High Efficiency Particulate Absorber.
Hepatitis B	A **prescribed disease** caused by a **virus** which produces inflammation of the liver. The **virus** is particularly resilient and resists common antiseptics and even boiling water, and can live in the environment for weeks. Occupations at risk are predominantly health care workers, teachers, police and customs officers who may be exposed to human body fluids.
Hepatoma	Liver tumour. See **Angiosarcoma**.
Hepatotoxic	Toxic to the liver.
Herzberg (Frederick)	Management guru of the 1950's whose main motivation theory recognised the differences between factors which satisfy and those which dissatisfy. His theory is known as the motivation/hygiene theory.

HFL	**Highly Flammable Liquid.**
Hierarchy of Needs	Motivation model offered by **Maslow** based upon five levels: 1. Food, warmth and shelter 2. Safety and security 3. Social needs and affiliation 4. Ego needs and self esteem **5. Self actualisation**
High Court	Trial venue for civil cases involving large claims (usually in excess of £50,000).
High Explosive	Explosive material possessing a high rate of decomposition which produces a pressure/**flame front** at high velocities, known as **detonation**.
High Pressure (electrical)	**Pressure** in a system (UK) normally above 650 volts, but not exceeding 3000 volts, where the electrical energy is used or supplied.
Highly Flammable Liquid	A (liquid) substance which has a flash point of less than 32°C.
HIV	Human Immunodeficiency Virus.
Hoist	A hoist is an appliance whose rotational movement is restricted by guides or rails. It can only move in the vertical plane.
Hold to Operate Control	Protective device which requires the operator's presence and action on the controls to allow the machine or equipment to operate. Releasing the controls causes the equipment to stop.
Holism	School of thought which suggests that activities or systems should be studied as a whole because they show **emergent properties** which cannot be predicted by the study of the behaviour of individual components.
Holistic Approach	See **Holism**.
Hook	A device used to secure a **load** to a **crane**.
Hot Wire Anemometer	Instrument for measuring air velocity comprising a very fine heated wire attached to the end of a probe. As air passes over the wire the wire cools and the rate of heat dissipation is directly proportional to the velocity of air passing over the wire.

House of Lords	The highest court in the land and the final (UK) **Court of Appeal** in both civil and criminal proceedings. A quorum of three judges is necessary but some major issues are decided by the whole House.
HSC	**Health and Safety Commission.**
HSE	**Health and Safety Executive.**
HSG48	**HSE** guidance publication entitled 'Reducing Error and Influencing Behaviour' useful for its insight into the effects of human behaviour on an organisation's management system, and vice versa. Read it.
HSG65	Successful Health and Safety Management: **HSE** publication detailing essential features of a safety management system. Read it.
Human Error	An action or decision which was not intended, which involved a deviation from an accepted standard, and which led to an undesirable outcome. See also **Errors**.
Human Error Probability	The probability that an error will occur during the performance of a particular job or task within a defined period of time (**HSG48**). See also **THERP**.
Human Factors[1]	Expression generally used to describe the outcome of human psychological processing influenced heavily by experience, knowledge, **perceptual set** and **motivation**.
Human Factors[2]	From the **HSE** - "human factors refer to environmental, organisational and job factors, and human and individual characteristics which influence behaviour at work in a way which can affect health and safety". The main elements are now contemporised in **HSG48** Reducing Error and Influencing Behaviour.
Human Failures	A hierarchy of human failures postulated by the **HSE** in **HSG48** which includes **errors** and **violations**.
Human Relations	School of management which proposed that people work better in groups where they have some degree of participation and control over their work. Relations within the group are more important than mechanistic controls applied by the employer.

Human Reliability

The propensity for a human being to perform a particular task to a specified level of performance. The probability that a task will be successfully completed within a required minimum time (**HSG48**). See **THERP**.

Human Reliability Analyses A collection of techniques, based upon **probabilistic risk assessment**, for predicting **human error**. See **THERP**.

Humidifier Fever

An allergy causing **alveolitis** resulting from exposure to bacteria and fungal spores which grow in water and are recirculated through humidifying systems. Workers in air conditioned offices are more likely to be affected.

Hybrid Offence

A criminal offence triable at either **Magistrates Court** (summarily) or **Crown Court** (on indictment) at the discretion of the prosecution or sometimes at the request of the defendant.

Hygiene

See **Occupational Hygiene**.

Hygiene Standard

Generic expression for limits of exposure to airborne substances. See **Occupational Exposure Limits**.

Hygienist

See **Occupational Hygienist**.

Hypoxia

A low blood tension of oxygen caused by a low inspired concentration of oxygen.

Iceberg Theory[1]

That insured costs of accidents represent only a small part of the total costs to a company and are thus the tip of the iceberg.

Iceberg Theory[2]

That major injury and lost time accidents represent only a fraction of the total number of accidents occurring in a company and are thus the tip of the iceberg.

ILO

International Labour Organisation.

Immediate Cause

The identifiable **unsafe act** or **unsafe condition** which existed immediately prior to the occurrence of an **accident**. See also **Root Cause** and **Basic Cause**.

Impedance

Is the opposition to flow of electrical **current** made up of **resistance** (a property of the material at specified temperature), **capacitance** and **inductance**.

Implied Term	A condition of a **contract of employment** that is implied rather than expressly included. Implied terms may be by statute (Working Time Regulations) or by common law (duty of care).
Improvement Notice[1]	Statutory notice which may be issued by an Inspector from the **HSE** or an **EHO** on discovery of a breach of one of the relevant statutory requirements. A time limit of at least 21 days must be given in which to comply or appeal to an **employment tribunal**.
Improvement Notice[2]	Statutory notice which may be issued by the fire authority on premises exempt from the requirement to hold a **fire certificate** on discovery of inadequate means of escape or fire fighting. A time limit of at least 21 days must be allowed in which to comply or appeal to an **employment tribunal**.
Impulse Noise	Any type of single or repeated noise of short duration, eg a hammer or power press.
Incendive	Having enough energy to ignite a flammable mixture.
Incidence Rate (IR)	Statistic used to illustrate the number of accidents (of a specified type) per 1000 employees (or other constant*)

$$IR = \frac{\text{Total number of Accidents}}{\text{Number of employed persons}} \times 1000$$

	*Note that the multiplier may vary for different organisations, agencies and countries. Use caution when making comparisons.
Incident	All undesired circumstances and "near misses" which could cause accidents (**HSG65**).
Independent Tied Scaffold	A **scaffold** whose structural support is provided by **standards**, **braces** and **ledgers** and is tied to the building using **scaffold ties**. The working platform rests on **transoms**.
Indictable Offence	Serious criminal offence for which higher penalties or longer terms of imprisonment may be applied (see s33 HASAWA).
Indirect Costs	Those costs associated with accidental losses which are not easily observed or directly associated with the accident. These include the cost of lost time by others involved in the event, investigation costs, loss of goodwill or corporate image, hiring or training of new staff etc. See also **Direct Costs**, **Insured Costs** and **Uninsured Costs**.

Indirect Discrimination   Where a provision, condition, criterion or practice which would apply equally to all persons would be detrimental to a larger proportion of people afforded protection under the legislation, eg placing conditions that would debar considerably more of a complainants group than the ordinary population.

Individual   See **Personality**.

Individual Differences   Human factors which give rise to propensity for a particular **attitude** or **behaviour** in an individual such as age, experience, maturity and **personality**.

Individual Risk   Term used when determining the tolerability of **risk** to define the **risk** to a member of the public living within a defined radius of a hazardous industrial installation. See **Societal Risk**.

Inductance   The property of an electrical circuit (**alternating current**) to impede the flow of **current** through the creation of an **electro-magnetic field** in the opposite direction of flow.

Industrial Tribunal   See **Employment Tribunal**. Title changed by the Employment Rights (Dispute Resolution) Act.

Inerting   A process of rendering a substance or atmosphere incapable of combustion.

Informal Group   Pattern of human interaction governed by personal needs rather than organisational requirements.

Informal Organisation   See **Informal Structure**.

Informal Structure   (of an organisation). The actual day to day relationships which develop to meet **individual** needs and satisfactions, in order to enable organisational and personal goals to be realised.

Infrared Gas Analyser   A **direct reading instrument** for gases which measures the amount of absorption of gas and compares it with a reference cell. Because different gases absorb infra-red at different wavelengths it is possible using this method to selectively analyse several gases even when present in the same.

Infrared Radiation   Invisible **electromagnetic radiation** of wavelength in the region of 760nm to 1nm. It occurs between the red end of the visible spectrum and the shortest microwaves. Its harmful effects on the human being include burning of the skin, increase in pigmentation and the induction of cataracts.

Injunction	A remedy in **common law** to prevent a threatened infringement of a **plaintiff's** property rights (either physical or intellectual).
Injury	See **Personal Injury**, **Major Injury** and **Over Three Day Injury**.
Inspection	See **Safety Inspection**.
Insulation[1] (Fire)	Relating to fire resisting properties - the ability of a structure to prevent the transfer of heat through the structure for a specified period of time when exposed to fire.
Insulation[2] (Noise)	A barrier to the transmission of noise.
Insulation[3] (Electrical)	A means of preventing direct contact with an electrical **conductor** by the use of a non-conductive material.
Insured Cost	Those costs associated with accidents which are covered by the payment of an insurance premium eg employers liability, buildings, plant, vehicles etc.
Integrated Pollution Control	A principle of the Environmental Protection Act which demands a cross media approach to controlling emissions from regulated or prescribed processes.
Integrating Sound Level Meter	A sound level meter which can accumulate the total sound energy over a period of time and give an average result.
Integrity	Relating to fire resisting properties - the ability of a structure to resist the passage of flame and hot gas for a specified period of time when exposed to fire.
Intelligence	The capacity of an individual to deal with the environment in a logical way demonstrating reasoning power, comprehension, speed, accuracy and communication ability.
Interlocked Guard	A protective device which renders a **machine** incapable of being started or becoming dangerous, prevents the guard from being opened whilst the **machine** is in a dangerous state, or brings a **machine** to a stop if the guard is displaced for any reason. May involve mechanical, electrical, pneumatic or hydraulic components or a combination of these. See **Power Interlocking** and **Control Locking**.

International Labour Organisation	A UN specialised agency which formulates international labour standards in the form of Conventions and Recommendations setting minimum standards of basic labour rights: freedom of association, the right to organise, collective bargaining, abolition of forced labour, equality of opportunity and treatment, and other standards regulating conditions across the entire spectrum of work related issues.
Involuntary Manslaughter	Where a death occurs but the accused had no intention (**mens rea**) of killing or seriously harming their victim.
Ion	An electrically charged **atom** or grouping of **atoms**.
Ionisation	The process by which a neutral **atom** or **molecule** acquires or loses an electric charge. The production of ions.
Ionising Radiation	A type of **radiation** which produces changes in atomic structure by causing an **electron** discharge in the **atom**. In the absence of the balancing **electron** the **atom** becomes positively charged and is called an **ion**, hence ionising radiation.
IOSH	Institution of Occupational Safety and Health, professional body which represents the professional and educational interests of **safety practitioners**. See **Registered Safety Practitioner**.
IPC	**Integrated Pollution Control.**
Irradiance	The power per unit area of **optical radiation**. Unit: Watt per square metre, symbol: $W\ m^{-2}$.
Irritant	A substance with the ability to cause irritation at point of contact with the body. See **Primary Irritant** and **Secondary Irritant**.
Isocyanates	See Appendix 2 Commonly Occurring Substances.
Isolation	A **control measure** useful for dealing with a toxic hazard in a work area where most of the other work is **risk** (chemical) free. The particular process which is dangerous can be segregated and special precautions can be taken in this area.

Isolation[1] (Noise)	A material or technique which prevents transmission of vibrational energy to adjoining structures.
Isolation[2] (Electrical)	The provision of a secure break in an electrical **conductor** capable of preventing the transmission of prospective fault currents.
Isotope	**Nuclides** with the same number of **protons** but different numbers of **neutrons**.
Job Safety Analysis	A procedure which identifies the **hazards** associated with each step of a job and develops solutions for each **hazard** that will either eliminate it or control it.
JSA	**Job Safety Analysis.**
Judicial Precedent	A judge-made decision given weight by the seniority of the court which made it, which has a binding effect on the future interpretation of similar legal issues heard in lower courts. See **Obiter Dictum** and **Ratio Decidendi**.
Jury	A body of 12 persons selected randomly from society challenged with the task of determining the guilt or otherwise of persons charged with a **crime**.
Kata Thermometer	An alcohol thermometer used to measure air speed or atmospheric conditions by means of cooling effect.
Knowledge-based Behaviour	When confronted with an unfamiliar situation with no, few, or partial rules available from past experience, a worker acts on their perception of the 'state of the world' and on some overall aim. Perceiving these 'symbols' induces the operator to develop a strategy using knowledge, reasoning and experience as a reflection of the goal generated. The strategy itself is selected and tested through a process of trial and error. See **Knowledge-based Mistakes**.
Knowledge-based Mistakes	In circumstances where known rules do not apply the operator will be less certain and decision making will involve far more conscious effort. This delivers many more ways in which information processing can fail, ie shortcomings of attention, working memory, logical deduction and decision making.

Laser	Device which amplifies **light** and usually produces an extremely narrow intense beam of a single **wavelength**. Light Amplification by a Stimulated Emission of Radiation.
LD_{50}	Stands for lethal dose 50, an index of acute toxicity established by dosing animals (usually rats) until 50% of the test population dies. Doses may be established for oral, dermal or inhalation exposures eg LE_{50}(concentration).
Lead	See Appendix 2 Commonly Occurring Substances.
Leadership	A social process in which one individual influences the **behaviour** of others without the threat of violence.
Learning	Relatively permanent changes in a person's **behaviour** as a result of experience. See **Classical Conditioning** and **Operant Conditioning**.
Ledgers	The horizontal metal poles which connect the outer and inner **standards** of a scaffold structure and support the **Transoms**.
Legionellosis	A type of pneumonia caused by the bacteria Legionella Pneumophila. The organism is usually transmitted in contaminated water aerosols. Occupational groups at risk include water system maintenance engineers and workers in air-conditioned buildings although many documented exposures of the general public exist.
Legionnaires Disease	See **Legionellosis**.
Legitimate Power	The ability to influence the **behaviour** of people because they believe you have a right to give orders and they are under an obligation to follow them.
$L_{EP,d}$	A measure of the average sound pressure level, measured in **dB(A)**, for the time period of a standard working day (ie 8 hours).
Leq	A measure of the average sound pressure level, measured in **dB(A)**, over any time period. Note: Leq of 8 hours is equivalent to L_{EPd}.
LEV	**Local Exhaust Ventilation.**
LFL	**Lower Flammable Limit.**
Licensed Waste Manager	One who is in possession of a licence under s34 of the Environmental Protection Act.

Lifting Accessories	Work equipment for attaching loads to machinery for "lifting". This definition includes: **slings**, **shackles**, swivel or **eyebolts**, clamps, lifting magnets and lifting beams.
Light	Visible **electromagnetic radiation** which directly causes visual sensation. The conventional wavelength limits of light are 380nm to 760nm.
Light Absorption Instrument	A **direct reading instrument** for particulates which compares the colour intensity of deposit against a standard.
Light Guard	See **Photo-electric Device**.
Light Scattering Instrument	A **direct reading instrument** for particulates based upon the **Tyndall beam** principle in which the air to be sampled is passed through an intense light beam. The light is scattered by the particles and the intensity and frequency of scattering is monitored by photo-multipliers which gives an instant readout of the number of particles in a given size range which, when related to the flow gives a number concentration for that size range.
Likelihood	A qualitative description of **probability** or frequency.
Liquid Adsorber	**Sampling head** which allows contaminated air to be drawn through a suitable solvent contained in a glass or plastic 'bubbler' or impinger. This technique is sometimes known as **solvent scrubbing**. See **Liquid Adsorption**.
Liquid Adsorption	Collection technique for airborne gas and vapour sampling which involves drawing air through a solvent medium contained in a sampling head. The gas or vapour present is adsorbed into the solvent and can then be analysed for substance identification and concentration levels.
Liquid-Solid (Absorption) Chromatography	The liquid mobile phase (ie mixture A and B) is passed through a column packed with silica gel or alumina. Liquid - Liquid (Partition) Chromatography. The mobile phase is passed over a thin layer of liquid held on the surface of a porous inert solid such as paper in water. The process is sometimes known as 'thin layer' or 'paper' chromatography. High Pressure Liquid Chromatography (HPLC). Separation is achieved by reducing the particle size of the stationary phase and forcing the mixture through at high pressure, hence HPLC.

Load	For **LOLER** this includes any material, people or animals that are lifted by lifting equipment.
Local Effects (Health)	The action of a **chemical**, **biological** or **physical agent** at the site of contact such as the skin, mucous membranes of eyes, nose, mouth, throat or respiratory or gastro intestinal tract.
Local Exhaust Ventilation	Mechanical extraction ventilation designed to intercept contaminants at source and remove them from the workplace before people are exposed to them.
Lock-off System	A device or procedure using one or more hasps and locks which achieves the physical isolation of electrical or mechanical power.
LOLER	Lifting Operations and Lifting Equipment Regulations
Loss	The net summation of **damage** and **personal injury** resulting from an **accident**.
Loss Control	A management system designed to reduce or eliminate all aspects of accidental loss which lead to a wastage of company or organisation assets. Any negative consequence of an **accident** event.
Loss Prevention	The application of engineering techniques in order to reduce accidents which result in personal injury and damage to property or products. (Institution of Chemical Engineers).
Low Explosive	Low explosive material whose propagation occurs by **deflagration** often producing large volumes of hot, smoky gas.
Low Pressure (electrical)	**Pressure** in a system (UK) normally not exceeding 250 volts where the electrical energy is used.
Lower Flammable Limit	The lowest concentration of fuel that will just support a self-propagating flame.
Lyme Disease	An arthritic condition associated with skin rashes, fever, and sometimes encephalitis caused by a spirochaete which is transmitted by a tick bite.
Lymphatic System	System in which **Lymphocytes** operate.
Lymphocyte	A cell, which forms part of the human immune system, which recognises antigens in the human body and manufactures antibodies, or deals directly with the antigen to combat the danger they present.

MAC	Russian **occupational exposure limit** defined as "Those concentrations of harmful substances in the air of the working area which will not cause any disease or deviation from a normal state of health of the workers or their offspring, detectable by current methods of investigation, either during the work itself or in the long term".
Machine	An assembly of linked parts or components, at least one of which moves, with the appropriate actuators, control and power circuits, joined together for specific application, in particular for the processing, treatment moving or packaging of material.
Macrophage	A large **phagocyte** found in many organs and tissues which moves between cells and use the scavenger properties to collect and remove foreign bodies.
Magistrates	Ordinary men or women generally possessing no formal legal training who are selected from the population and appointed to act as peer judges of those accused of **summary offences**. See also **Stipendiary Magistrate**.
Magistrates Court	Venue for the adjudication of less serious criminal offences. As a court of trial between three and seven **Magistrates** try **summary offences** specified by particular statutes (eg s33 HASAWA). Penalties and punishments are limited by statute.
Maintenance	The activity of keeping equipment and facilities in a safe and reliable condition so that they can perform their function efficiently.
Major Accident	An occurrence such as a fire or emission or explosion resulting from uncontrolled developments in the course of an industrial activity which presents a serious risk to persons inside or outside the installation, or damage to the environment.
Major Hazard[1]	A general but imprecise term used to describe large scale industrial installations which have the potential for a **major acciden**t eg chemical or nuclear plants. Certain installations are specified in regulations.
Major Hazard[2]	A large scale industrial hazard whose realisation involves significant event, often a breach of containment.
Major Injury	A notifiable **injury** of a kind specified by regulation (**RIDDOR**) eg fracture of a major bone, amputation, loss of consciousness etc.

MAK	German **occupational exposure limit** defined as "The maximum permissible concentrations of chemical compounds in the air within a working area which, according to current knowledge, generally do not impair the health of employees nor cause undue annoyance".
Man Sievert	See **Collective Effective Dose**.
Management Oversight and Risk Tree (MORT)	An analytical technique developed in the nuclear industries which employs a formal, disciplined logic or decision tree which relates and integrates a wide variety of safety concepts systematically. It is based on the principle that accidents arise from either management oversights or assumed risks and develops fault paths along these lines.
Manometer	Device used for the accurate measurement of air pressures within a ventilation duct.
Manslaughter	Where a death has occurred but the wrongful act leading to it falls short of murder. See **Voluntary Manslaughter** and **Involuntary Manslaughter**.
Maslow Abraham	Management guru who proposed a dynamic concept of human motivation in the form of a **hierarchy of needs** which takes account of both personality variables and the process of social change.
Mass Number	The number of **protons** plus **neutrons** in the **nucleus** of an **atom**.
Maximum Exposure Limit	The maximum concentration of an airborne substance, averaged over a reference period, to which employees may be exposed by inhalation under any circumstances. Control measures must be applied to reduce exposures as low as is reasonably practicable without resorting to **PPE**. See **ALARP**.
Maximum Permissible Exposure (radiation)	The **irradiance** likely to cause detectable damage to the human eye or skin from exposure to **optical radiation**. Unit: Watt per square metre, symbol: W m^{-2}.
Mayo (Elton W)	Management guru of the 1930's who was a proponent of the **human relations** school of management.
MBOCA	**Methylene-bis-o-chloraniline.**

Mean Duration Rate (MDR) A statistic used to illustrate the average number of days lost per accident (of a specified type).

$$MDR = \frac{\text{Total Number of Days Lost}}{\text{Total Number of Accidents}}$$

Mean Radiant Temperature The thermometer is housed in a black copper sphere(150mm) and allowed to come into equilibrium with the environment. It is possible to get an accurate measurement of MRT by calculation (complex!) or the use of a nomogram.

Means of Escape Structural measures by which a safe route or routes are provided for persons to travel from any point in a building to a place of safety. See **Alternative Means of Escape**.

Mechanical Hazards Machinery hazards classified by BS EN 292 including: crushing, shearing, cutting, entanglement, drawing - in, impact, stabbing, friction and abrasion, and high pressure fluid/ejection amongst others.

Medical Surveillance Health surveillance under the supervision of a qualified medical practitioner. Certain requirements are specified by legislation eg **CoSHH** schedule 5.

Medium Pressure (electrical) **Pressure** in a system (UK) normally above 250 volts, but not exceeding 650 volts, where the electrical energy is used.

MEL **Maximum Exposure Limit.**

Mens Rea A defined state of mind attributable to a person in the causing of the **actus reus**, - the guilty mind.

Mercury 'Sniffer' A **direct reading instrument** which draws contaminated air into an absorption chamber where it is exposed to ultraviolet light at 254nm. Mercury tends to absorb UV radiation and the degree of absorption if mercury is present is directly proportional to the concentration.

Mesothelioma A notorious form of **cancer** associated with exposure to **asbestos** especially in the form of **crocidolite**. It can occur at even small exposures with a latency period of up to 40 years. Mesothelioma is a **prescribed disease** and also reportable under **RIDDOR**.

Metabolic Rate The rate of energy produced per unit area over the body.

Metabolism	A mainly beneficial process occurring in the liver, kidneys, lungs and skin which converts a toxic substance to a non-toxic one or vice versa eg: the skin converts some constituents in tar into carcinogens.
Methylene-bis-o-chloraniline	See Appendix 2 Commonly Occurring Substances.
MHSW	The Management of Health and Safety at Work Regulations.
Micron	A unit of measurement, one thousandth of a millimetre, one millionth of a metre (0.000001m).
Micro-organism	A microbiological entity, cellular or non-cellular which is capable of replication or of transferring genetic material.
Mist	Liquid droplets suspended in air. Usually generated by the condensation from the gaseous to the liquid state or by dispersing a liquid through agitation or atomizing.
Mitigation	Arguments put forward by the defendant after a guilty plea, or after being judged guilty, which promote extenuating circumstances or other favourable conditions in an attempt to minimise the penalty imposed.
Mobile Crane	A self propelled crane whose body is supported on a wheeled chassis. The jib is usually capable of rotating 360° and extending substantially to deliver loads in awkward places. Stability is provided by outriggers that should be lowered before a lift is attempted.
Molecule	The smallest portion of a substance that can exist by itself and retain the properties of the substance.
Mond Index	A way of ranking chemical plant hazards similar to the **Dow Index**. It takes account of circumstances other than processing, such a storage, loading and unloading. Toxicity hazards are also included.
Motivation	A decision-making process through which the individual selects desired outcomes and sets in motion the behaviours appropriate to acquiring them. Motivation has three main components: energising, directing and sustaining.
mppcm	Millions of particles per cubic metre, a numerical measure for dusts and other particulate matter.

Mucociliary Escalator	The lining of the upper airway which consists of microscopic hairs on the lining cells covering mucous membranes. Their activity maintains the movement of fluid over these membranes.
Multi Causality Theory	Modern trend in **accident** investigation and analysis which accepts the principle that accidents are usually the result of a number of interrelated causes, none of which can be described as the sole cause. The concept leads to a systems approach to accident investigation and prevention rather than the concentration on one specific causal relationship.
Mutagen	A substance which if inhaled, ingested or penetrates the skin may produce a risk of hereditable genetic defects ie a permanent change in the amount or structure of the genetic material which results in a change to the characteristic of the daughter cells.
Mutagenesis	A permanent change in the amount or structure of the genetic material (the 'genotype') which results in a change to the characteristics of the daughter cells (the 'phenotype').
Mutation	A chemical change in the **DNA** in the **nucleus** of a cell. Mutations in sperm or egg cells or their precursors may lead to inherited effects in children. Mutations in body cells may lead to effects in the individual.
Narcosis	A condition of profound insensibility resembling, but not the same as, sleep.
Narcotic	A chemical substance which has the potential to cause the onset of sleep or even **narcosis**.
Narrow Band Noise	The division of the frequency content of a particular noise into bands of a fixed width.
Near Miss	An accident event which does not realise its potential for injury or damage. See **Incident**.
NEBOSH	National Examination Board in Occupational Safety and Health which develops syllabuses at professional and general levels and sets examinations for each in occupational safety, health and environment. See **NEBOSH Certificate** and **NEBOSH Diploma**.
NEBOSH Certificate	Vocational qualification aimed at managers and others who carry special or designated responsibilities for health and safety in a workplace.

NEBOSH Diploma	Professional vocational qualification aimed at those pursuing a career in occupational health and safety. It is an accepted entry qualification for **IOSH**.
Negligence	"The omission to do something which a **reasonable man**, guided upon those considerations which ordinarily regulate the conduct of human affairs, would do, or doing something which a prudent and **reasonable man** would not do" (Blythe v Birmingham Waterworks Co 1856)
Neighbour Principle	"You must take reasonable care to avoid acts or omissions which you can reasonably foresee would be likely to injure your neighbour. Who then is my neighbour? Persons who are so closely and directly affected by my act that I ought reasonably to have them in contemplation as being so affected when I am directing my mind to the acts or omissions which are called in question". (Lord Atkin in Donoghue v Stevenson 1932).
Neighbour Test	See **Neighbour Principle**.
Neoplasm	A "new growth". A term associated with the growth of tumours in body tissue. See **Cancer**.
Neoplastic Disease	See **Cancer**.
Nephrotic Syndrome	Characterised by massive protein loss and consequent oedema of the face and dependant areas, especially the ankles.
Neutron	An elementary particle with unit **atomic mass** approximately and no electric charge.
Newtonian Behaviour	The behaviour of large particles in air as they set up turbulence and eddies and are greatly affected by drag. The resistance of the air is proportional to the square of the velocity and the square of the diameter of the particle.
Noise	Subjective description given to unwanted **sound**.
Noise Assessment	The determination of the noise exposure of a person or a group of persons. A legal requirement under the Noise at Work Regulations 1989 where the noise level is likely to be greater than or equal to the **first action level**. Or greater than or equal to the **peak action level**.
Noise Exposure	A measure of the total sound energy to which a person is exposed, dependant upon duration of exposure and **sound pressure level**.

Noise Rating Curves	A family of curves which are basically a set of **octave band** spectra, each with its own rating number. The NR rating is the highest NR curve touched. The NR curves were developed in Europe and are internationally standardised and are essentially consistent with the US Equivalent Noise Criteria (NC) curves.
Noise Refuge	See **Acoustic Haven**.
Noise Survey	A preliminary activity prior to a full **noise assessment** which looks at noise levels at specified locations in a work area.
Non-destructive Testing	Any form of testing which does not result in permanent damage or deformation to the part being tested. Eg x-ray inspection, gamma radiography, magnetic crack detection and dye penetration.
Non-ionising Radiation	Radiation falling within the upper range of the **electromagnetic spectrum** which does not have the capacity to cause ionisation eg infra red and ultra violet.
Non-mechanical Hazards	Machinery hazards classified by BS EN 292 including: noise, vibration, electricity, high/low temperatures, radiation and hazardous substances.
Non-pecuniary Damages	**General damages** for which there is no formal monetary scale of award such as pain and suffering, social isolation etc.
Notifiable Disease	A disease prescribed by the Public Health (Infectious Diseases) Regulations 1998 eg tetanus.
Nuclear Reactor	A device in which nuclear **fission** can be sustained in a self-supporting chain reaction involving **neutrons**. In thermal reactors, **fission** is brought about by thermal neutrons.
Nucleus	The positively charged core of an **atom** which occupies little of the volume but contains most of the mass.
Nucleus of a Cell	The controlling centre of the basic unit of tissue which contains the **DNA**.
Nuclide	A species of **atom** which is characterised by the number of **protons** and **neutrons** and, in some cases, by the energy state of the **nucleus**.

Nuisance	See **Public Nuisance, Private Nuisance** and **Statutory Nuisance**.
Nuisance Noise	A **noise** which is unlikely to cause hearing damage but which is annoying to those in the area.
Obiter Dictum	Remarks made by judges in the summing up of a case which are 'by the way' and not essential elements of the decision itself. These remarks often become persuasive precedents depending upon the seniority of the judge but they are not part of the **ratio decidendi**.
Objective Measures	**Performance measures** which are detached from the observer's personal judgement eg existence of 'X' in fact.
Obstructive Airway Disease	See **Occupational Asthma**.
Occupational Asthma	A disorder of breathing characterised by a narrowing of the airways due to swelling of the airway wall. The condition is triggered by occupational exposure to **allergens** and some chemical substances.
Occupational Exposure Limit	A level of exposure expressed as an **OES** or **MEL** which is used to determine the adequacy of control of exposure by inhalation in the workplace. OELs are specified in official guidance EH40.
Occupational Exposure Standard	The concentration of an airborne substance, averaged over a reference period, at which, according to current knowledge, there is no evidence that it is likely to be injurious to employees if they are exposed by inhalation, day after day, to that concentration.
Occupational Hygiene	The practice of recognition, measurement, evaluation and control of occupational health risks.
Occupational Hygienist	One who practices **occupational hygiene**.
Octave Band	The division of the frequency range of **noise** into bands with the upper frequency of each band being twice that of the lower frequency.
Octave Band Centre Frequency	The frequency at the centre of an **octave band**. Used as a point in the measurement of noise.
OEL	**Occupational Exposure Limit.**
OES	**Occupational Exposure Standard.**

Off The Job Training	**Training** which takes the trainee away from the distractions of work activity into a formal classroom environment.
Official Journal	Official journal of the **European Union** in which a **directive** is published once it has been adopted.
Off-line Processing	The mental simulation of the choices open to us and their possible outcomes which has the disadvantage that we sometimes fail to consider properly all the options, or may not have sufficient information to enable us to make a choice.
Ohm's Law	The potential difference between the ends of a **resistance** (or conductor) is directly proportional to the **current** flowing - assuming constant temperature. This relationship is given by the equation: **Voltage = current x resistance.**
Oil Acne	Skin infection developing from plugged pores which become infected and produce blackheads and pustules. Dirty work involving mineral oils can lead to its development particularly on forearms and thighs.
On The Job Training	**Training** which takes place in the workplace at the trainee's workstation usually whilst engaged in normal duties.
On-line Processing	Moment to moment decision making which requires little analysis of the outcomes but has the disadvantage that an inappropriate choice may be made on the spur of the moment.
Open Face Head	**Sampling head** which accommodates filters of 25 and 37 mm diameter for sampling general or 'nuisance' dusts where high concentrations of larger sized particles are expected. Open face with cowl is more likely to be seen sampling for asbestos. The cowl protects the face of the filter and gives even distribution of airflow.
Open System	A system that interacts with and depends upon exchanges with its environment. A flexible and adaptive **system**.
Operant Conditioning	A learning process observed by Skinner in which appropriate or desired behaviour is rewarded when it is observed thus making it more likely that the behaviour be repeated.

Optical Radiation	**Electromagnetic radiation** comprising **ultraviolet**, **visible** and **infrared radiations**.
Organisation	The arrangement of human and physical resources based upon the need to control and integrate the activities of **individuals** and **groups**.
Over Three Day Injury	A notifiable injury which causes absence from work or the inability to perform normal duties for a period of more than 3 days excluding the day of the injury but including rest days (**RIDDOR**).
Overhead Travelling Crane	Overhead (or gantry) cranes run on tracks which span the workshop. They are often capable of withstanding high stresses but all of the components must be taken into account when assessing strength. This includes the tracks on which the crane runs and the points at which they are fixed to the building structure.
Oxidising Agent	A chemical substance which promotes a combustion reaction when mixed with a combustible material.
Ozone	A form of oxygen gas which occurs naturally in very small quantities in air. Most of the ozone is in the stratosphere where it forms the ozone layer.
Ozone Detector	A **direct reading instrument** unique to **ozone** which works on the principle of chemiluminescence. Air is drawn into a reaction chamber where the **ozone** (if present) is reacted with ethylene. The product of this is in a high energy state and rapid return to its ground state occurs with the emission of light. This emission is amplified and measured.
P4SR	**Predicted Four Hour Sweat Rate**.
Paper Tape Monitor	A **direct reading instrument** for vapour which involves exposing a roll of chemically treated paper tape to a flow of contaminated air. As the air filters through the tape the paper stains black in the presence of the contaminant. The tape advances until the stain is directly above a light source where a detector picks up the amount of light transmitted through the paper (light varies according to the depth of stain).
Parallel System	A **reliability** engineering technique in which the capabilities of a critical component are duplicated so that if one fails the other is capable of continued operation, eg dual circuit braking system.

Parasites	Multi-cellular organisms with complex life cycles growing, for example, from egg to larva to adult which depend upon larger organisms for survival.
Particle Motion	The behaviour of dusts and fibres of various sizes in air. See **Newtonian Behaviour**, **Stokes Behaviour** and **Brownian Motion**.
Particulate Radiation	Sub-atomic particles emitted from a radio-active material which cause ionisation in the absorbing medium. See **Alpha Radiation** and **Beta Radiation**.
Parts Per Million	Units of measurement for **volumetric** concentration of airborne contaminant.
Pascal (Pa)	Unit of measurement of sound pressure.
Passive Sampler	A device used to collect air samples without the aid of a pump. **Gas** is adsorbed or absorbed by the collecting medium at a rate of diffusion across a well defined diffusion path.
Pathogen	An organism which can infect a host and cause disease.
Peak Action Level	A point at or above which an employer must take action to reduce the noise exposure of the workforce by means other than **PPE**. A **peak sound pressure level** of 200 pascals (at time of going to print).[2] See also **First Action Level** and **Second Action Level**.
Peak Sound Pressure Level	The maximum value reached by the sound pressure at any instant during a measurement.
Pecuniary Damages	**General damages** for which there is a formal monetary scale of award such as insurance scales for fracture and amputation, loss of future earnings etc.
Peer Group	The group to which an **individual** belongs.
Peer Group Pressure	The pressure exerted by a group (sometimes coercive) on its members to ensure compliance with the group's values and norms.
Perceived Risk	The level of risk as valued by non-experts, which is often influenced by subjectivity and personal judgement as to the potential disturbance of things that they value.

---

[2] The forthcoming updated Noise at Work Regulations is likely to reduce the PAL to 140 pascals.

Perception	A psychological process by which we make sense of what we are experiencing.
Perceptual Distortion	A type of error created by the altered perception of data because of the way the information is presented.
Perceptual Set	A characteristic **filter** pattern, which develops through experience, which allows some information to pass through the **filter** more readily.
Performance Measures	Key outcome indicators based upon an organisations stated objectives in OH&S. See **Qualitative Measures**, **Quantitative Measures**, **Subjective Measures** and **Objective Measures**.
Performance Monitoring	A process by which an organisation determines its success or failure in managing OH&S. See **Proactive Monitoring** and **Reactive Monitoring**.
Permanent Threshold Shift	Permanent irreversible hearing loss occurring after prolonged exposure to high noise levels. See **Temporary Threshold Shift**.
Permit to Work	A formal authority to operate a planned procedure which is designed to protect personnel working in hazardous areas or activities.
Peroxidation	A slow reaction of a peroxidisable chemical with air to form peroxides which may separate or crystallise to form an explosive or even detonative component.
Person Culture	A style of organisational behaviour described by Charles **Handy** which strives to meet the needs of individuals. Often associated with government driven services.
Personal Injury	Any disease or impairment of a person's physical or mental condition (**HASAWA** s53). See **Major Injury** and **Over Three Day Injury**.
Personal Protective Equipment	All equipment (including clothing affording protection against the weather) which is intended to be worn or held by a person at work and which protects a person against one or more risks to their health and safety.
Personal Sampling	The collection of samples of airborne concentrations of **substances hazardous to health** by attaching a small collector in the **breathing zone** of the worker under observation.

Personality	A word used to describe that collection of behaviour that makes one person distinguishable from another. A collection of attributes including **intelligence**, **aptitude**, **attitude**, experience, memories, knowledge and skills.
Phagocyte	A cellular defence mechanism which recognises unfamiliar cells, cell debris and particles etc in the human body and digests them in order to render them harmless.
Photo-electric Device	Protective (trip) device utilising a beam or beams of light (usually infrared) between a light source and a photo-sensitive cell. If the beam is broken power to the machine is automatically made safe.
Photon	A quantum of **electromagnetic radiation**.
Physical Agent	In the context of health and safety a physical hazard in the form of **noise**, **vibration** or **radiation** which has the potential to cause harm.
Physical Hazard	See **Physical Agent**.
Piezo Balance	Dust measurement instrument which gives a direct mass concentration readout. A crystal is set up in oscillation and the rate of oscillation is influenced by the amount of dust deposited on it.
Pitot Tube	An open ended tube which is connected to a **manometer** with the other end placed in the airflow enabling total pressure to be measured.
Pitot-static Tube	A combination of a **pitot tube** surrounded by a second tube which provides static pressure measurements.
Plaintiff	An injured or aggrieved person making a claim under **civil law**. See **Claimant**.
Planning Supervisor	A **competent person** appointed by the **client** under **CDM** reg 6 whose role is to ensure the competence of **designers** and **contractors** before they are appointed. One of the main duties of the Planning Supervisor is to ensure that a **Health and Safety Plan** for the project is prepared before construction work starts.
Plenum Ventilation	Mechanical form of **dilution ventilation** (from the Latin plenus meaning full).

Pluralist	A **frame of reference** based upon the premise that **conflict** is normal and to be expected between two parties, the balance of power shifting between one and the other depending upon the circumstances.
Pneumoconiosis	A **prescribed disease** of the lungs caused by exposure to inhaled dust, commonly found in mineworkers but many other occupational sources are listed. It is a generic description given to a range of diseases which include **asbestosis**, **silicosis** and coalworkers pneumoconiosis. Also reportable under **RIDDOR**.
Policy	See **Safety Policy**.
Polluter Pays Principle	The polluter bears the expenses of carrying out the pollution control measures decided upon by public authorities to ensure that the environment is in an acceptable state (Organisation for Economic Cooperation and Development).
Pollution	The release into any environmental medium from any process or substances which are capable of causing harm to humans or any other living organisms supported by the environment.
Population Potential	The number of people that could be affected by an accident.
Positron	See **Beta Particle**.
Potential Difference (Electrical)	Measured relative to some fixed point in an electric field usually at earth potential (zero). Before a **current** will flow from one point to another say point A to point B, then A must have a higher potential than B. The unit of potential difference is the **volt**.
Power	The ability to get things done by threat or force or sanction. See also **Coercive Power**, **Expert Power**, **Legitimate Power**, **Referent Power** and **Reward Power**.
Power Culture	A style of organisational behaviour described by Charles **Handy** which is based upon power emanating from central 'Zeus like' figures.
Power Interlocking	A safeguarding system for machinery in which the movement of the guard is interlocked with the direct switching of the power to the **hazard**.
PPE	**Personal Protective Equipment.**

PPM	See **Parts Per Million**.
PRA	**Probabilistic Risk Assessment.**
Practicable	A stricter duty than 'reasonably practicable' in which the cost of precautions is not a factor. Something is practicable if it is possible to be accomplished with known means or resources and feasible within the scope of current knowledge and invention.
Precautionary Principle	Environmental measures must anticipate, prevent and attack the cause of environmental degradation. Where there are threats of serious or irreversible damage, lack of full scientific certainty should not be used as a reason for postponing measures to prevent environmental degradation (UN Economic Commission for Europe).
Predicted Four Hour Sweat Rate	An index based on the concept that the sweat rate is an adequate index of heat stress. Its value is nominally the amount of sweat secreted by fit, acclimatised young men exposed to the environment for four hours. The stress is therefore directly measured by the strain it produces (in this case sweat!).
Predicted Noise Level	The noise reduction to be expected based upon **attenuation** data supplied by the manufacturers of noise reduction equipment or materials.
Prescribed Disease	A disease of occupational origin which is prescribed by regulations under the Social Security Act, and qualifies for Industrial Disablement Benefits. (The Social Security [Industrial Injuries] [Prescribed Diseases] Regulations).
Prescriptive Legislation	Statutory codes which specify exactly the conditions for compliance and often the means by which they should be achieved.
Pressure (electrical)	Electrical **Potential**. See **Low Pressure**, **Medium Pressure**, **High Pressure**, **Extra-high Pressure**.
Primary Explosion	See **Explosion**.
Primary Group	Small **group** developing within a larger system with the objective of satisfying the affiliation needs of **individuals** within it. They are relatively intimate, informal and based upon personal relationships rather than roles conferred by the **organisation**.

Primary Irritant	A substance causing an **irritant** effect on the skin by direct action eg acids, solvents and detergents.
Principal Contractor	The **contractor** who undertakes or manages the construction work for the **client**.
Private Nuisance	An unlawful and continuing interference with a persons use or enjoyment of land.
Proactive Monitoring	See **Active Monitoring**.
Probabilistic Risk Assessment	An assessment which identifies potential routes to an undesired consequence and assigns probability data to the causal paths so as to produce a quantified estimate of the **risk**.
Probability	The likelihood of a specific event or outcome (usually expressed as a number between 0 and 1) measured by the ratio of actual events to the total number.
Prohibition Notice[1]	A statutory notice which may be issued by an inspector of the **HSE** or an **EHO** which requires the recipient to cease or not to begin an activity. The notice is served where an inspector forms the opinion that the activity presents a risk of serious personal injury. A breach of statute is not necessary and the notice remains in force during the period of any appeal.
Prohibition Notice[2]	Statutory notice which may be issued by the fire authority on premises which present a serious risk to persons in the event of fire. The notice may prohibit the use of or restrict the use of premises until appropriate remedial action is taken.
Prosecute	The act of initiating and pursuing a legal action before the criminal courts.
Prospective Fault Current	The maximum **current** which may flow in a system when there is a short circuit or an earth fault.
Protected Disclosure	A disclosure of information made in the public interest as a **qualifying disclosure** under The Public Interest Disclosure Act.
Protected Face Head	**Sampling head** which accommodates a 25 mm dia filter and is protected by a cover plate with a single hole which generates a higher capture velocity and is useful for collecting heavier metals eg lead, cadmium.

Protected Route

A route leading to an exit from a floor or to a final exit which is separated from the remainder of the building by walls, partitions, doors, floors and/or ceilings of fire resisting construction.

Protective Device (electrical)

A device such as **fuse, earth, RCD, reduced voltage transformer**, etc, designed to reduce the risks associated with electrical systems.

Proton

An elementary particle with unit **atomic mass** approximately and unit positive electric charge.

Psittacosis

A **reportable disease** of the **zoonose** type brought on by exposure to infected droppings, dust or feathers and infected tissues in birds. Exposure can cause respiratory infection.

Psychology

A branch of the **behavioural sciences** concerned with the observation, explanation and prediction of individual behaviour.

Psychrometer

An instrument for measuring atmospheric humidity utilizing a dry and wet-bulb thermometer and whirled manually or by motorized unit to provide the moderate air flow necessary to obtain an aspirated wet-bulb temperature reading.

Public Nuisance

The interference with the use or enjoyment of a property or facility by the public in general, so widespread in its range, so indiscriminate in its effects that it would be unreasonable to expect one person to take steps to put a stop to it. It may constitute a criminal offence as well as allowing a civil action to anyone who may be harmed.

Pulmonary Oedema

A waterlogging of the lungs.

Putlog Scaffold

A **scaffold** whose structural support is provided by **putlogs**. The working platform rests on the **putlogs**.

Putlogs

Metal scaffold tubes flattened at one end into a spade like shape and inserted into brickwork.

PUWER

The Provision and Use of Work Equipment Regulations.

Pyrophoric Compounds

Materials which are so reactive that contact with air or moisture causes oxidation or hydrolosis so rapidly that the heat evolved is sufficient to cause ignition.

QRA

Quantified Risk Assessment.

Qualifying Disclosure	A disclosure made to a specified person or body which a worker reasonably believes tends to show: that a criminal offence has been committed; a failure to comply with a legal obligation has occurred; a danger to health and safety exists; damage to the environment; or a miscarriage of justice has taken place etc.
Qualitative Measures	**Performance measures** that are descriptions of situations or conditions which cannot be recorded numerically.
Quality	Conformance to specification.
Quantified Risk Assessment	Process of assignment **risk** to an event using numerical and probabilistic data. Often applied to large scale industrial operations which present **major hazards**.
Quantitative Measures	**Performance measures** that are described in terms of numbers, eg on a scale. The number of lost time accidents.
Quantum of Risk	The amount of **risk**, comprising qualitative and quantitative elements, based upon a number of factors such as **probability** or chance of an event occurring; the number of occasions a person is exposed to the **hazard**; the number of people affected by a single event; and the maximum probable loss likely to be experienced (among others).
Radiation	The emission of radiant energy in the form of particles or waves. See **Ionising Radiation** and **Non-ionising Radiation**.
Radiation Protection Advisor	A person appointed by a radiation employer to ensure compliance with regulatory requirements.
Radiation Protection Supervisor	A person appointed by a radiation employer to oversee compliance with local rules.
Radical	A **frame of reference** usually associated with a basic power imbalance which is permanent rather than transitory. Those without power always seeking to overthrow those with power.
Radioactive	Possessing the property of **radioactivity**.
Radioactive Waste	Useless material containing **radionuclides** which is categorised in the nuclear power industry according to **activity** (and other criteria) as low level, intermediate level, and high level waste.

Radioactivity	The property of **radionuclides** of spontaneously emitting **ionising radiation**.
Radiofrequency Radiation (RF)	**Electromagnetic radiation** used for telecommunications and found in the **electromagnetic spectrum** at longer **wavelengths** than **infrared radiation**.
Radiological protection	The science and practice of limiting the harm to human beings from **radiation**.
Radionuclide	An unstable **nuclide** that emits **ionising radiation**.
Rasmussen	Author of "Skills, Rules & Knowledge: Signals, signs & symbols, and other distinctions in human performance models" which identified three important types of behaviour: **skill-based behaviour**, **knowledge-based behaviour** and **rule-based behaviour**.
Ratio Decidendi	The reasoning in a particular case which was essential to reaching the decision and forms the binding **judicial precedent**.
Raynaud's Disease	Medical description of naturally occurring white finger resulting from exposure to cold, in this sense also referred to as Primary Raynaud's disease. See **Vibration White Finger**.
RCD	**Residual Current Device.**
Reactive Monitoring	Activity directed towards detecting and analysing failures in an organisation's OH&S management system.
Reactive Silencer	An expansion box for pressure waves whose size, length and cross section area, can be chosen so as to selectively attenuate at certain frequencies. The larger the area, the higher the attenuation whilst the length generally dictates the frequencies attenuated.
Reasonable Care	The **common law** standard of care expected by the **reasonable man**. It combines the processes of reasonable foresight (was the defendant's behaviour a reasonably foreseeable cause of loss); and reasonable alternative (were there reasonable precautions open to the defendant that would have prevented the loss).

Reasonable Man	Archaic description given to a hypothetical being who is neither imprudent nor overcautious. A judge adopts this role impartially when determining whether or not the **defendant** has been negligent.
Reasonably Practicable	The legal standard classically defined in the case of Edwards v NCB 1949 where the quantum of risk involved is placed upon one scale and the cost of the measures necessary for averting the risk are placed upon the other. Where the costs far outweigh the risks involved it is not reasonably practicable to do more. See **Practicable**.
Recurrence Potential	The inherent potential of an **accident** to repeat itself.
Reduced Voltage Transformer	A device used to reduce mains (UK:230 volts) **voltage** to a lower level eg 110 volts. The **earth** is fixed to the centre of the 110v side giving a maximum **voltage** of 55v in the event of a fault occurring.
Reductionism	A scientific procedure which reduces the complexity of a **system** to simpler and more manageable components with the objective of isolating a single component to control it or eliminate all the factors except the one that influences it. The basic assumption is that the response of the component to variations in its influencing factor is representative of the component when it is in the **system**.
Reductionist Approach	See **Reductionism**.
Redundancy	A **reliability** engineering technique which involves duplicating parts in a **system** so that if one part fails the other is capable of maintaining the integrity of the **system** on its own.
Reference Group	A **group** to which an **individual** does not belong but nevertheless has attributes, facilities and conditions which an **individual** finds desirable. The **individual** makes reference to these things in the process of setting demands and aspirations.
Referent Power	The ability to influence the **behaviour** of people because one has characteristics that are desirable and that they should follow. Sometimes known as charisma.
Registered Safety Practitioner	A safety professional who is a member of **IOSH** and has demonstrated sufficient competence through education and experience to be included on the Register of Safety Practitioners.

Regulation	A statutory device approved by Parliament made under a general provision in an Act of Parliament, sometimes called delegated or subordinate legislation. Regulations often identify specific risks and set out specific action that must be taken. Regulations often contain absolute legal standards not qualified by the term reasonably practicable. See **European Regulation** and **Statutory Instrument**.
Reinforcement	A necessary component in the **learning** process which rewards required **behaviour** (positive reinforcement) or punishes inappropriate **behaviour** (negative reinforcement).
Relative Humidity	The ratio of the vapour pressure existing to the saturated vapour pressure for the same dry bulb temperature.
Relativistic Risk Assessment	An assessment which ranks a risk in relation to other risks.
Reliability	The probability that an item will perform a required function under stated conditions for a stated period of time. (See **Human Reliability**).
Reliability Data	Data used to define the sustained performance achieved by components in a system, or an entire system, and their propensity to break down.
Reportable Disease	A disease specified in schedule 3 of the Reporting of Injuries Diseases and Dangerous Occurrences Regulations.
Representative of Employee Safety	A person elected to represent fellow employees for the purposes of consultation with the employer in matters of health and safety. Statutory provisions are housed in the Health and Safety (Consultation with Employees) Regulations. See **Safety Representative**.
Res Ipsa Loquitur	'The thing speaks for itself' - a legal phrase applied in circumstances where there can be no other explanation for the occurrence of an event other than the defendant's negligence.
Residual Current Device	This is an electro-mechanical protective system, it provides physical isolation of the live and neutral conductors when a sensor detects a different **current** flowing along the neutral compared with the live.

Resistance (R)	The 'frictional' opposition to a flow of electric **current** measured in ohm's.
Respirable Dust	Dust of less than 10 **microns** which is capable of penetrating deep into the **alveoli**, (source BSEN 481). See **Total Inhalable Dust** and **Thoracic Dust**.
Respirator	**Respiratory protective device** which purifies air by drawing it through a filter medium which removes most of the contaminant. Not to be used in oxygen deficient atmospheres.
Respiratory Protective Device	A device falling into the category of **respiratory protective equipment**. See **Respirator** and **Breathing Apparatus**.
Respiratory Protective Equipment	Generic name given to any equipment to be worn by a worker which prevents or reduces the inhalation of airborne contaminants.
Respiratory Sensitiser	A substance which can induce changes in the immune system of susceptible workers such that respiratory symptoms will present themselves on future exposure to the substance even at very low doses. This may lead to **occupational asthma**.
Responsible Person[1]	In the context of a **permit to work system**, the person undertaking the work in question who is bound by the conditions and requirements of the permit.
Responsible Person[2]	The manufacturer or importer of a product into the European Economic Community.
Retinal Burns	Eye injury caused by exposure to infrared radiation and lasers. Retinal burns and tears produce irreversible damage to that area of vision (blind spots).
Reveal Tie	A method of fixing a **scaffold** to a permanent or existing structure which involves wedging or jacking a tube tightly into the opposing faces of a window opening.
Review	The final component of a safety management system which involves the periodic revisiting of previous activity in health and safety in order to determine whether or not the standards set and achieved are still appropriate, eg a review of risk assessments.
Reward Power	The ability to influence the behaviour of people because they believe you are able to provide the benefits they desire. See also **Coercive Power** and **Expert Power**.

RIDDOR	Reporting of Injuries, Diseases and Dangerous Occurrences.
Ring Tie	A method of fixing a **scaffold** to a permanent or existing structure which involves fixing a ring to the outside of the structure and securing the **scaffold** with wire or steel ties.
Risk[1]	The probability of a consequence of particular severity arising out of exposure to a hazard, usually associated with adverse outcomes (John Gilbertson). See **Acceptable Risk**, **Assessed Risk**, **Estimated Risk**, **Tolerable Risk** and **Unacceptable Risk**.
Risk[2]	The likelihood that a specified undesired event will occur due to the realisation of a hazard (**HSG65**).
Risk Analysis	The process of discovery of predisposing **risk**, associated with disciplines (eg **ergonomics**) where individual **susceptibility** is an overriding factor.
Risk Assessment	The process of identifying and evaluating the risks associated with exposure to a particular hazard. Process now prescribed by various legislation including the Management of Health and Safety at Work Regulations. See **Generic Risk Assessment** and **Quantified Risk Assessment**.
Risk Avoidance	The conscious decision on the part of an organisation to avoid a particular risk by discontinuing the hazardous operation which gives rise to it.
Risk Control	The application of technical, procedural and behavioural measures to reduce **risk**.
Risk Control Systems	Systems put in place to ensure the provision and continued operation of **workplace safety precautions**, eg (for **PPE**) purchasing standards, issue, training, maintenance and storage arrangements.
Risk Estimation	A component of **risk assessment** based upon objective or quantitative data such as failure rates, **reliability** data, experience etc.
Risk Evaluation	A component of **risk assessment** based upon subjective or qualitative data influenced heavily by the perceptions and experience of the observer.

Risk Management[1]	The systematic process of identification, evaluation and subsequent control of risks. The object is to reduce the impact of **risk** on the business as a whole.
Risk Management[2]	The process which achieves the most efficient combination of controls necessary to provide reassurance that business objectives can be achieved reliably. - **Turnbull Report**.
Risk Phrase	A concept introduced by the Chemicals (Hazard, Information and Packaging for Supply) Regulations. Chemicals possessing specified risk characteristics must be labelled with the relevant risk information (phrase) eg R45; may cause **cancer**.
Risk Reduction	A strategy applied after techniques of **risk avoidance**, **risk transfer**, and **risk retention** have been undertaken. Involves application of safety and loss prevention techniques to protect company from **indirect** and **uninsured costs**.
Risk Retention	Usually a conscious decision on the part of a company to retain a **risk** within its financial operations. This may involve the formation of a captive insurance company or, more usually, the acceptance of a voluntary excess.
Risk Transfer	Conventional use of third party to take **risk** on one's behalf. eg use of insurance company or by contract.
Robens Report	Watershed report of a Government committee of inquiry into health and safety at work chaired by Lord Robens. Its findings and recommendations in 1972 were immediately followed by the introduction of the Health and Safety at Work etc Act 1974.
Role	The way individuals express themselves within the context of those around them. Specific **behaviour** patterns which conform to the expectations of others, eg father/husband; wife/mother; boss/subordinate; teacher/students.
Role Ambiguity	A condition experienced when the **role** offered to us does not match our **expectation** of it.
Role Conflict	A condition experienced when an **individual** is confronted with the simultaneous existence of two or more sets of role **expectations** where compliance with one makes it difficult to comply with others eg boss/friend.

Role Culture	Euphemism for the more pejorative expression **bureaucracy** offered by management guru Charles **Handy**. A culture bound by rules and procedures and managed by officialism.
Root Cause	The underlying cause or causes of an **accident** which exist as weaknesses or failures in a company's management system, described in some texts as **basic causes**.
Rotameter	A float type measuring device used for the on site calibration of a **sampling train** immediately prior to and after the **sampling** period.
Rotating Vane Anemometer	Instrument used for measuring air velocity comprising a disc of angled vanes attached to a rotating spindle. The speed at which the vane assembly rotates when placed in the airflow is a measure of the air velocity acting upon it.
Route of Entry	In **occupational hygiene**, the route of entry into the body of a substance hazardous to health. The routes of entry in order of importance are inhalation, ingestion, absorption and injection.
Routine Monitoring	Regular **sampling** programme applied in conditions where employee exposures are significant but below the **exposure limit** and rising, or not as low as is **reasonably practicable**.
Routine Violation	A **violation** which, through custom and practice, has become the norm. A disastrous example of this (Herald of Free Enterprise) was the leaving open of the bow doors on cross channel ferries until the journey was underway so as to reduce the time in port. See **Situational Violation** and **Exceptional Violation**.
RPE	**Respiratory Protective Equipment.**
RSI	Repetitive strain injury. An out of favour expression coined in the 80's to describe conditions now included in the collective description **work related upper limb disorders**.
RSP	**Registered Safety Practitioner.**
Rule-based Behaviour	On recognition of certain cues indicating the environmental state(s) a worker will use learned rules or procedures. These rules may be derived through experience (trial and error) or may be communicated through training. See **Rule-based Mistakes**.

Rule-based Mistakes	Where the operator is familiar with the situation (or believes that they are) and evokes a plan of action to deal with it. The choice of the rule(s) follows an 'if...then' logic. If their understanding of the environment or conditions matches the 'if' part of the rule or when the rule has been used successfully in the past, the 'then' part is activated, sometimes in the wrong circumstances.
Safe System of Work	A formal procedure designed to eliminate or control hazards which includes the physical layout of the job, the sequence of operations, provision of tools and equipment and the issuance of relevant notices, warnings and specific instructions. A planned procedure to prevent harm to personnel.
Safety	The minimisation of contact between a person and **hazard**, predominantly concerned with the prevention of physical harm to an **individual**.
Safety Assurance	The concept that safety can be managed in a similar way to quality assurance, by following management systems designed to eliminate accidents. The concept was at its height in the mid 1980s but has been largely superseded by **HSG65** and **BS8800**.
Safety Audit	A systematic and critical examination of each area of a company's activity, the object of which is to reduce accidents and minimise loss. The process not only looks for the presence of a safety related activity but also how well it is carried out.
Safety Case	A systematic and often quantified model of a system or installation which demonstrates that it meets specified safety criteria. It is a legal requirement in certain industries such as offshore workings, nuclear power generation and the operation of railways.
Safety Climate	The environment in which a **safety culture** thrives or otherwise, indicated by the number of accidents and failures, attitudes of management, presence of policies and procedures etc.
Safety Culture[1]	The set of norms, roles, beliefs and attitudes, and the social and technical practices within an organisation, which are concerned with minimising exposure to hazard and risk. (John Gilbertson).

Safety Culture[2]

"The safety culture of an organisation is the product of individual and group values, attitudes, perceptions, competencies, and patterns of behaviour that determine the commitment to, and the style and proficiency of, an organisation's health and safety management. Organisations with a positive safety culture are characterised by communications founded on mutual trust, by shared perceptions of the importance of safety and by confidence in the efficacy of preventative measures". (HSC's Advisory committee on the Safety of Nuclear Installations).

Safety Data Sheet

Information sheet relating to a chemical supplied with intention of being used at work. Required by virtue of **CHIP** the information to be included is specified in the schedule to the regulations.

Safety Factor

See **Factor of Safety**.

Safety Inspection

An examination of a work area against a pre-determined checklist which seeks to identify **substandard conditions** and **acts**.

Safety Management System

An integrated combination of policies, procedures, codes and rules which dictate how the company responds to the safety demands placed upon it. A framework for management decision making which helps to clarify any areas of ambiguity.

Safety Phrase

A concept introduced by the Chemicals (Hazard, Information and Packaging for Supply) Regulations. Chemicals requiring specified safety precautions must be labelled with the relevant safety information (phrase) eg S20: avoid contact with skin.

Safety Policy

A fundamental component of an organisations OH&S management system established by statute (HASAWA s2(3)). Three main elements include a statement of intent, organisational means for implementation, and the arrangements made for OH&S in the workplace. **MHSWR** added the requirement to include arrangements for assessing and recording significant risks.

Safety Practitioner

Evolutionary title now given to one who practises the discipline of occupational safety and health (see **RSP**). A practitioner is one who can identify symptoms of problems in an organisation; determine the cause; and deliver a remedy (John Gilbertson).

Safety Representative	A worker representative appointed by a recognised trades union in a workplace who has rights to perform statutory functions such as inspections, accident investigation, attend safety committee etc (Safety Representatives and Safety Committees Regulations). See also **Representative of Employee Safety**.
Safety Sampling	A routine, repeatable technique used to measure the **accident** potential of a particular area against a predetermined list of unacceptable deviations from standards.
Safety Survey	A detailed examination of critical areas of operation or particular operations or departments within an organisation eg machinery guarding survey, fire precautions survey.
Safety Tour	An impromptu, unscheduled examination of a work area to review a particular subject or issue. Undertaken by, for example, safety committee at an appropriate juncture or a supervisor or manager in response to a problem etc.
Sampling[1]	See **Safety Sampling**.
Sampling[2]	The measurement and analysis of general and personal exposure to hazardous substances in order to evaluate compliance with **occupational exposure limits**.
Sampling Head	The working end of a **sampling train** which holds the sample collection medium. See **Open Face Head**, **Protected Face Head, Cyclone Head, Solid Adsorber** and **Liquid Adsorber**.
Sampling Train	The set of equipment used for **personal sampling** for airborne concentrations of **substances hazardous to health**, comprising a **filter, sampling head**, flexible tubing and a portable pump.
Scaffold	A temporary working platform constructed of sound, strong materials, usually metal tubes. See **Putlog Scaffold, Independent Tied Scaffold** and **Birdcage Scaffold**.
Scaffold Tie	A method of fixing a **scaffold** to a permanent or existing structure. See **Reveal Tie, Through Tie** and **Ring Tie**.
Scaffold Tower	A portable **scaffold** structure comprising of prefabricated sections which can be easily transported and fitted together at a worksite. They are frequently fitted with castor wheels for ease of movement in place.

Scientific Management	A school of management developed between 1910 and 1940 which was based upon a logical and rational approach with an emphasis on making people work more efficiently by breaking down large tasks into smaller components and clearly defining how the job should be done and how long it should take. See **Taylor**.
Scintillation Counter	A device containing material that emits **light** flashes when exposed to **ionising radiation**. The flashes are converted to electric pulses and counted. The number of pulses is related to **dose**.
Second Action Level	A point at which an employer must take action to reduce an employees exposure to noise by means other than personal protection where **reasonably practicable**. A **daily personal noise exposure** of greater than or equal to 90dB(A) (at time of going to print).[3] See also **First Action Level** and **Peak Action Level**.
Secondary Explosion	An **explosion** of dust layers and deposits which have been disturbed by a smaller **primary explosion**.
Secondary Group	A large, relatively **formal group** such as a department or section within an **organisation**. **Role** relationships are predominant and the **group** functions impersonally at a fairly instrumental level.
Secondary Irritant	A substance whose reaction on the skin occurs some time after repeated exposure and occasionally the effects may be observed on parts of the body other than those originally exposed. Condition is also known as **allergic dermatitis**.
Selectivity	A function of human perceptual processing which either consciously or unconsciously allows the brain to recognise signals or data from the environment. We 'see', 'hear' etc what we want to.
Self Actualisation	A state of self fulfilment which emerges when lower order needs have been satisfied, described by **Maslow** as a degree of autonomy and choice about self and a release of potential.

---

[3] The forthcoming updated Noise at Work Regulations is likely to reduce the SAL to 85dB(A)$L_{EP.d}$.

Self Regulation	Modern trend in safety legislation which sets standards and objectives and leaves it to the duty holder to determine how best to achieve them.
Semiconductor Chemisorption Detector	A **direct reading instrument** for organic gases in which the contaminant is chemisorbed onto a metal oxide surface causing a change in the electrical resistance of the semiconductor material. The change in resistance is proportional to the concentration of **gas**.
Sensitiser	See **Respiratory Sensitiser** and **Allergic Dermatitis**.
Sensory Illusion	A type of error experienced through sensory perception when information received confuses sensory receptors eg very cold substances appear hot, glass doors appear invisible because of lighting.
SEPA	Scottish Environmental Protection Agency.
Severity Potential	The worst injury, illness or damage that could result from an accident.
Severity Rate (SR)	Statistic used to illustrate the average number of working days lost due to accidents for every 100,000 hours worked.

$$SR = \frac{\text{Total Number of days lost}}{\text{Total person hours worked}} \times 100,000$$

Note: that multiplier may vary for different organisations, agencies and countries, use caution when making comparisons.

SFAIRP	So far as is reasonably practicable. See **Reasonably Practicable**.
Shackles	A device in the shape of a bow or the letter D incorporating a removable bolt which can be attached to an **eye bolt** or part of a fixture to create a lifting point.
Short Term Exposure Limit	The 15 minute **TWA** exposure which should not be exceeded at any time during a work day even if the daily **TWA** is not exceeded. It is designed to take into account the acute effects of short term high exposure to chemicals.
Sievert	See **Effective Dose**.
Silencer	See **Reactive Silencer** and **Absorptive Silencers**.

Silica	See Appendix 2 Commonly Occurring Substances.
Silicon Diode	A device made of a silicon compound in which current flows when exposed to **ionising radiation**. The current is converted to electrical pulses and counted. The number of pulses is related to **dose**.
Silicosis	A **prescribed disease** of the lungs characterised by the development of fibrotic modules around the embedded **silica** dust. The disease gradually develops as large coalescent nodules reduce lung function and cause breathing difficulties.
Simple Asphyxiant	A substance which causes suffocation by reducing the amount of oxygen available in the atmosphere for gas transfer in the lungs; examples include nitrogen and carbon dioxide. See **Chemical Asphyxiant**.
Single European Act	In 1986, a European Union Treaty which set out the conditions and mechanisms for European integration by the end of year 1992.
Situational Violation	A **violation** where the rules are broken due to pressure to complete the task, or because it is difficult to comply with the rule in the circumstances, e.g. a scaffolder not using a harness because there is no where to secure it at that time. See **Routine Violation** and **Exceptional Violation**.
Six Pack	Reference to six sets of regulations brought into force by the end of 1992 to meet targets for a particular phase of European unification. The expression is no longer of significance due to the many changes which have taken place since their introduction.
Skill-based Behaviour	Is displayed in familiar situations where the operator recognises a signal, understands that this requires a normal routine and therefore executes a well learned and practised response more or less automatically. See **Skill-based Errors**.
Skill-based Errors	May be considered as intention (of outcome) being correct but the action (motor-response) is executed badly. Examples include pressing the wrong button on a telephone or computer keyboard where the consequences are relatively trivial - however, pressing the accelerator instead of the (intended) brake in a driving emergency may be a more costly slip.

Skin Ulceration	The result of exposure to hexavalent chromium (eg: cement burns and chrome holes) and, in extreme form, in perforation of the nasal septum (work in plating shops).
Sling	Flexible equipment constructed from **chain**, **fibre rope** or **wire rope** used to lash or secure loads to lifting devices.
Societal Risk	Term used when determining the tolerability of risk to define the chance of a large accident in a hazardous industrial installation causing a defined number of deaths or injuries. See **Individual Risk**.
Sociogram	A diagrammatic or mapping technique used to display the interpersonal preferences of members of a **group** ie. who likes who, who works best with..., who is the preferred leader etc?
Sociology	A branch of the **behavioural sciences** concerned with theories and predictions about complex social **groups**, the differences between them and structural influences upon them.
Socio-Technical System	Concept of an **organisation** which illustrates the interdependency of its technical components (task and technology) and its social components (structure and people).
Sodium Hydroxide	See Appendix 2 Commonly Occurring Substances.
Soft System	A **system** comprising of mainly abstract things, thus strongly dependant upon the **perceptions** of the observer.
Sole Plates	Long boards placed under the **base plates** of **standards** whose purpose is to evenly distribute the weight of the **scaffold**.
Solid Adsorber	**Sampling head** comprising a glass tube containing an adsorbent material such as powdered charcoal or silicon gel. The material effectively adsorbs **vapours** from the air passing over it and after **sampling** the tube is sealed and sent for analysis.
Solvent Scrubbing	Alternative name for **Liquid Adsorption**.
Sound	Any pressure variation (in air, water or other medium) which is detectable by the human ear.
Sound Power Level	A measure of the total acoustic power produced at the **noise** source.

Sound Pressure Level	The basic measure of **noise**, at a distance from the noise source, expressed in **decibels** usually measured with a **frequency** weighting eg **dB(A)**.
Special Damages	**Compensation** consisting of calculable **damages** generally prior to a case being heard which include legal and medical expenses, loss of earnings and costs of adjustments to lifestyle.
Specific Gravity	The weight of a liquid relative to water, values of less than one indicate that a material will float on water.
Spectrophotometry	A technique used for measuring or comparing the absorbencies of solutions, gases or vapours. A monochromatic beam of **light** is passed through a sample which may transmit or absorb or scatter the light in some way. The remaining **light** is measured as an output by a photometer.
SPL	**Sound Pressure Level.**
Spontaneous Combustion	A condition manifesting in certain materials (especially organic materials) which react with oxygen at room temperature and produce heat. If the fuel is a good insulator the heat generated builds up until the **autoignition temperature** is reached and true combustion commences.
Spontaneous Ignition Temperature	See **Autoignition Temperature**.
Spurios Trip	A fault which causes a system to activate when not required.
Stability	Relating to fire resisting properties - the ability of a structure to resist collapse for a specified period of time when exposed to fire.
Stack Effect	Method of ventilating a building using the principles of convection. Heated air inside the building is discharged through a chimney (stack) and cool outside air is drawn in through windows or vents to replace it.
Stain Tube Detector	A proprietary device comprising a chemical reagent housed in a glass tube. Air is drawn through the tube by means of a pump and any contaminant in the atmosphere causes the reagent to change colour. The length of colour stain in the tube is proportional to the concentration of contaminant in the atmosphere.

Standard	The long upright metal poles which constitute the vertical structure of a **scaffold**.
Standby System	A reliability engineering technique involving the installation of a secondary unit which activates upon the failure of the primary unit.
Static Pressure	The difference between the absolute pressure at a point in an airstream or pressurised chamber and the absolute pressure at ambient temperature (ie the bursting pressure).
Statute Law	A source of law in the form of a codified, written structure laying down formal rules to be observed by those to whom the statute is expressly or implicitly addressed. The laws are interpreted by the courts and such interpretations are binding on lower courts. Breaches of statute are normally, but not always, concerned with criminal law. For instance the Occupier's Liability Acts give rights in civil law only. A **breach of statutory duty** may also give rise to civil liability unless the statute specifically excludes it.
Statutory Duty	Duty placed upon an individual by an **Act of Parliament** or **Regulation**.
Statutory Instrument (SI)	Official description given to subsidiary or **delegated legislation** which puts in effect specific duties which are described in general terms in the parent Act, eg SI 1992 no 3073 The Supply of Machinery (Safety) Regulations 1992.
Statutory Nuisance	One specified by statute for which there are specified courses of action by either an individual or an **enforcement authority**.
STEL	**Short term exposure limit.**
Stereotype	An **expectation** held by most of the population of either a person or situation.
Stimulus Response Learning	Lower order state of learning in which the learner exhibits behaviour directly related to a specific stimulus. See **Classical Conditioning** and **Operant Conditioning**.
Stipendiary Magistrate	A **Magistrate** who is a qualified barrister or solicitor appointed to try cases in the **Magistrates Court**. Such persons are paid (a stipend) for their services and have the equivalent power of three lay magistrates.

Stoichiometric Mixture That mixture of fuel and oxidising agent (**vapour/gas**) which will combust completely. For hydrocarbon fuels in air, that mixture which combusts completely to produce carbon dioxide and water. There will be no fuel or oxygen remaining eg $CH_4 + 2O_2 \longrightarrow CO_2 + 2H_2O$ is a stoichiometric mixture; 1 part methane to 2 parts oxygen.

Stokes Behaviour The streamlined flow of smaller particles whose resistance in air is proportional to the diameter of the particle and its velocity.

Strain[1] Is the measure of the change in shape (or size) of a material when a force is applied in tension or compression.

$$\text{Strain} = \frac{\text{Change in length}}{\text{Original length}}$$

Strain[2] The physical or psychological manifestation of the effects of being exposed to **stress**. Symptoms may include **behaviour** changes or changes in **personality**.

Stress[1] Mechanical stress is the measure of the force applied to a body or component divided by the area over which the force is applied.

$$\text{Stress} = \frac{\text{Force}}{\text{Cross Sectional Area}}$$

Stress[2] An event or situation which places increased demand upon a person's mental or emotional resources. Sources of stress may be occupational or domestic/social each has the ability to be either stimulating or harmful. See **Strain[2]**.

Strict Liability Liability for an occurrence which does not require proof of **mens rea** only the **actus reus** needs be shown. The burden of proof rests with the **defendant**.

Stroboscopic Effects A phenomenon more usually associated with older lighting systems where the frequency of oscillations in light output is a multiple of the frequency of the movement of machinery. The **visual illusion** of stillness is created.

Subjective Measures **Performance measures** that are (or may be) influenced by the observer ie personal judgement may be subject to experience, knowledge or other influence.

Subordinate Legislation	See **Regulation**.
Substance Hazardous to Health	Defined by regulations as one which is very toxic, **toxic, irritant, harmful** or **corrosive**; **carcinogens**; **dust** of any kind in substantial concentrations; **micro-organisms**; and anything similar to the above.
Substandard Act	A term offered by Frank **Bird** in an attempt to objectify and define a measurable component of an **unsafe act**.
Substandard Condition	A term offered by Frank **Bird** in an attempt to objectify and define a measurable component of an **unsafe condition**.
Substitution	A **control measure** employed when elimination is impossible which substitutes a hazardous material for a less hazardous one, to substitute the state or form of the same substance for one which gives rise to less exposure.
Sub-system	An identifiable element of a **system** which has all the characteristics of a **system** in its own right.
Sue	The act of pursuing a legal claim in **civil law**.
Suitable and Sufficient	Often used concept in **goal setting legislation** which will ultimately be for the courts to decide. Broken down the word suitable suggests appropriate (in all the circumstances) for the purpose; and sufficient suggests of the right quantity, or going into enough detail to achieve compliance. Suitable and sufficient work equipment would imply the provision of the right tools, of the right quality, in sufficient quantities to enable work to be carried out safely.
Summary Dismissal	A situation where the employer terminates the employee's **contract of employment** without notice. In order to justify the use of this tactic the employee must be in breach of an important **express** or **implied term** of the **contract** such as gross misconduct.
Summary Offence	Less serious criminal offence normally tried in the **Magistrates Court**. Penalties are limited by statute (see s33 **HASAWA**).
Survey	See **Safety Survey**.
Susceptibility	The predisposition of a person to suffer a particular effect from exposure to a workplace condition or substance.

Synergy	Interaction between two or more components of a **system** which produces an output greater than that anticipated from the single addition of the individual outputs.
System	An assembly of component parts connected together in an organised way for the purpose of doing something. The components are affected by being in the system and the behaviour of the system changes if they leave it. See **Hard System**, **Soft System**, **Open System** and **Closed System**.
System (electrical)	See **Electrical System**.
Systematic	An organised, structured way of doing something.
Systemic	An analytical or investigative approach which considers a system as a whole with **emergent properties**.
Systemic Effects (health)	The action of a **chemical** or **biological agent** at a site remote from the point of contact after the substance has been absorbed.
Target Organ	The primary site of attack in the human body of a particular chemical or substance.
Task Culture	A style of organisational behaviour offered by Charles **Handy** which describes a lively, ad-hoc, versatile approach oriented to the task.
Taylor (Frederick W)	Management guru of the early 1900's who was a proponent of the school of **scientific management**.
Technical File	A collection of specified information and documentation listed in a product directive which includes: drawings, test results, calculations, a list of the relevant **essential health and safety requirements** and **EU** standards. The technical file need not exist per se, but must be capable of being assembled at the request of the **enforcement authority**.
Technique of Operations Review (TOR)	Analytical failure tracing technique based upon key phrases which, when identified as relevant, direct the user to other relevant causal factors for consideration. Its main strength is that it always directs the user away from 'fault of person' and considers management system failures instead.

Temporary Threshold Shift A temporary condition of hearing loss occurring immediately after exposure to high noise levels. See **Permanent Threshold Shift**.

Teratogen A substance which if inhaled, ingested or penetrates the skin, may involve a risk of subsequent non-hereditable birth defects in offspring.

Terminal Velocity The constant velocity of a particle falling freely in still air achieved when the force exerted by gravity is equal to the resistance imposed by the air.

Thermal Conductivity Detector In sample analysis, uses a hot wire or a thermistor as the sensing device. The readout is based upon the heat transfer from the hot filament to a cooler surface as the gas conducts heat from the filament to the wall. The amount of electrical energy supplied to the filament remains constant so any change in temperature (of the filament) will be a function of the thermal conductivity of the gas and its concentration.

Thermal Runaway Heat production at a rate which exceeds the ability to provide cooling. It can occur in a reaction because: as the temperature increases, the rate at which heat is removed increases linearly, but the rate at which heat is produced increases exponentially. Temperature can rise rapidly with little time for correction.

Thermoluminescent Material Irradiated material which releases **light** in proportion to the **ionising radiation** absorbed when it is subsequently heated.

THERP Techniques for Human Error Rate Prediction - the objective is to predict human error probabilities in order to evaluate their effect on the operating system as a whole.

Third Party A person not employed by an organisation but who interacts with it in some way, eg a contractor, member of the public, lawful visitor or even trespasser.

Thoracic Dust Dust of less than 10 microns in diameter which will escape the filtering effects of the nose and mouth and reach into the lungs. See Total **Inhalable Dust** and **Respirable Dust**.

Threshold Limit Value USA equivalent to our **occupational exposure limits** often referred to in hazard or chemical data sheets, (especially imports from USA). Warning <u>not</u> UK currency.

Through Tie	A method of fixing a **scaffold** to a permanent or existing structure which relies on a tube placed vertically inside a window opening and fixed to the **scaffold** outside by means of a tie tube.
Time Weighted Average	The average concentration of airborne contaminant measured over a normal 8 hour workday and 40 hour work week to which nearly all workers may be repeatedly exposed, day after day, without adverse effect.
Tinnitus	Involuntary sensation of noises in the ear such as buzzing or ringing, often associated with exposure to high noise levels.
TLV	**Threshold Limit Value.**
Toe Board	A board fixed at the lip of a working platform intended to prevent the falls of materials over the edge of the platform.
Tolerable Risk	A level of risk which is deliberately run for the benefit which is gained from running it. See also **Acceptable Risk** and **Unacceptable Risk**.
TOR	**Technique of Operations Review.**
Tort	A civil wrong for which the remedy is a common law action for unliquidated **damages**, and which is not exclusively the breach of a **contract** or the breach of a trust or other merely equitable obligation.
Tortfeasor	The person responsible for committing the tort.
Total Inhalable Dust	Dust of less than 100 **microns** diameter capable of entering the nose and mouth during normal breathing, (Source BSEN 481). See **Thoracic Dust** and **Respirable Dust**.
Tour	See **Safety Tour.**
Tower Crane	These feature heavily on the skylines of most cities and are constructed in situ from prefabricated sections. The long jib is counterbalanced by cantilevers or concrete blocks.
Toxic	A designation given to a substance which presents a serious hazard to health which is able to produce injury at a site in or on the body.
Toxicology	The study of the nature and action of poisons.

Training	A planned systematic process designed to modify **attitude**, knowledge, skill or **behaviour** through learning. See **On the Job** and **Off the Job Training**.
Transom	The metal pole set between the outer **ledger** and the inner **ledger** of a **scaffold** which supports the working platform.
Transport Velocity	The velocity of air flowing through a **local exhaust ventilation** system required to keep an airborne contaminant in suspension until it reaches the **air cleaning device**.
Transposed Harmonised Standards	A **EU** standard which has been agreed by **CEN** and identically worded throughout the member states in order to ensure that no state can block the importation of products meeting that standard.
Travel Distance	The actual distance a person must travel between any point in a building and the nearest door to a **protected route** or a final exit in the event of fire.
Trend Analysis	Visual representation of accident performance over a period of time, typically over monthly, quarterly and yearly periods. Conclusions drawn from the patterns illustrated should take account of any variables during the period under review such as number of hours worked, changes in staffing levels, production levels etc.
Trespass	A type of **tort**. See **Trespass to Land**, **Trespass to Goods** and **Trespass to Person**.
Trespass to Goods	The unlawful physical interference with another person's goods.
Trespass to Land	The unlawful entry, remaining, or deposit of a material object(s) on another person's land.
Trespass to Person	The assault, battery or false imprisonment of a person.
Trespasser	A person who has no lawful right to be in the place they are.
Tribunal	See **Employment Tribunal** and **Employment Appeal Tribunal**.
Trichloroethylene	See Appendix 2 Commonly Occurring Substances.
Trip Device	A protective device which detects the presence or entry of a person into the **danger zone** and cuts power to the machine eg antenna, pressure sensitive mat, photo-electric beam etc.

Turnbull Report Report of a working party led by Nigel Turnbull giving guidance on **risk management,** internal control and **corporate governance** for companies listed in the Stock Exchange. Now considered universally applicable (in principle) to any company seeking to improve its **risk management**.

TWA **Time Weighted Average.**

Two Handed Control A protective device which requires a machine operator to activate two start controls simultaneously before the machine will operate, the object being to keep the operator's hands out of the **danger zone**.

Tyndall Beam A very strong light source which presents an effective method of showing up the dispersion in atmosphere of **respirable dust** or **fume** not normally visible to the naked eye.

Type Approval Examination of a product by an **EU** approved body which confirms that the product type conforms fully with **transposed harmonised standards**.

UDS **Unit Density Sphere.**

UFL **Upper Flammable Limit.**

Ultra Vires Latin term used to describe any condition or situation in which a person has acted outside the powers conferred upon them by law. "Outside the law".

Ultraviolet Radiation **Electromagnetic radiation** in the wavelength range of 1nm - 380nm whose harmful effects on the human being include: burning of the skin, skin cancers, inflammation of the conjunctiva, and irritation of the cornea.

Unacceptable Risk A risk which is beyond the region of tolerability. See **Tolerable Risk**.

Unconfined Vapour Cloud Explosion See **Vapour Cloud Explosion**.

Unfair Dismissal A **dismissal** is unfair when the reason for it is 'inadmissible' eg activity relating to membership of a trade union, pregnancy or maternity, certain health and safety grounds, making a **protected disclosure** etc. See **Wrongful Dismissal**.

Uninsured Costs	Those costs associated with accidents which are not covered by normal insurance eg first part of a claim (excess), sick pay, time off, over time payments, investigation costs etc. See also **Direct Costs**, **Indirect Costs** and **Insured Costs**.
Unit Density Sphere	An assumed 'ideal' (spherical) particle having the same density as water, falling in still air, used for calculating theoretical values for **terminal velocity**.
Unitary	A **frame of reference** in which both parties share the same views. There is no conflict of interest.
Unsafe Act	An element of unsatisfactory behaviour immediately prior to an accident event which is significant in initiating the event. A **hazard** eg risk taking, short cuts, carelessness, lack of attention, horseplay etc. (John Gilbertson).
Unsafe Condition	An unsatisfactory physical condition existing in the workplace environment immediately prior to an accident event which is significant in initiating the event. A **hazard** eg slippery floor, broken glass, unguarded machine, trailing cable, low lighting levels etc (John Gilbertson).
Upper Flammable Limit	The highest concentration of fuel that will just support a self propagating flame.
Urticaria.	A hypersensitivity response, mediated by histamine, leading to wheals and flares (like nettlerash). Hair, urine and dander can cause it in small animal laboratory work; potato, fish and fruit preparation are responsible in catering.
UVCE	**Unconfined Vapour Cloud Explosion**. See **Vapour Cloud Explosion**.
Vane Anemometer	See **Rotating Vane Anemometer**.
Vapour	Gaseous form of substance which exists as a liquid (usually) under normal conditions.
Vapour Cloud Explosion	An explosion occurring outdoors beginning with the unplanned release of a large quantity of flammable **gas** or vapourising liquid which ignites following the formation of a cloud or plume of pre-mixed fuel and air. The speed of flame travelling through the cloud may approach **detonation** velocity with a massive pressure rise. The over pressure created causes initial damage to property.

Vapour Density	The ratio of a **vapour** or **gas** in relation to air which is taken to have a unitary value.
Vapour Pressure	The pressure exerted as a proportion of ambient pressure at a specified temperature (normally 20°C).
VCE	**Vapour Cloud Explosion.**
VCM	See **Vinyl Chloride Monomer**.
Velocity Pressure	The pressure increase produced by bringing a moving airstream to rest eg as measured by a **Pitot-static Tube**.
Velocity Profile	Graphical illustration of the behaviour of air currents around the opening of an **LEV** hood.
Ventilation	See **Local Exhaust Ventilation** and **Dilution Ventilation**.
Vibration	Mechanical oscillation produced by regular or irregular movements of a body about its resting position.
Vibration Dose	Magnitude of vibration x duration of exposure.
Vibration White Finger	A **prescribed disease** caused by exposure to vibrating hand held machinery characterised by episodic blanching of the middle or proximal phalanges or the proximal phalanx of the thumb. In this sense, also referred to as secondary **Raynaud's Disease**. **Vibration** causes spasm of peripheral blood vessels.
Vicarious Liability	Liability of one person for the behaviour of another acting on their behalf. The liability of the employer, for example, for the negligent acts or omissions of their employees acting within the cause and scope of their employment.
Vinyl Chloride Monomer	See appendix 2 Commonly Occurring Substances.
Violations	A deliberate deviation from a rule or procedure which may be **routine**, **situational** or **exceptional**.
Violence	"Any assault in which an employee is threatened or assaulted by a member of the public in circumstances arising out of the course of his or her employment" **HSE**.
Virus	Very small agents containing genetic material and a protein coat. They multiply using the mechanism of a host cell.

Visual Illusion	See **Sensory Illusion**.
Vitiligo	Alterations in skin pigmentation resulting from contact with chemicals eg Quinones which can destroy melanocytes causing patches without pigment
Volenti Non Fit Injuria	'No harm can be done to a willing person' - a legal phrase used to describe the willing participation of the **plaintiff** or **claimant** in the circumstances which led to their injury.
Volt	Unit of **potential difference**.
Voltage	See **Pressure**.
Volumetric	Term used to express concentrations of gases and vapours eg **parts per million** (ppm) (usually at 25°C and 760 mm pressure) - or as a percentage 1,000 ppm = 0.1%.
VWF	**Vibration White Finger.**
Waste	Any item which would ordinarily be described as waste, which is scrap material or discarded or being dealt with as if it were waste effluent or other unwanted surplus material, or something required to be disposed of as broken, worn out, contaminated or otherwise spoiled.
Waste Carrier	A person who transports **controlled waste** within the UK.
Waste Holder	A person who imports, produces, carries, keeps, treats, or disposes of **controlled waste** or, as a broker, has control of such waste.
Waste Manager	See **Licensed Waste Manager**.
Waste Producer	One whose actions give rise to the production of controlled waste.
WATCH	Working Group on the Assessment of Toxic Chemicals. An official working party which assesses toxicological data, epidemiology studies and other data relating to chemical substances in order to recommend appropriate control limits.
Wavelength	The distance between successive crests of an electromagnetic wave passing through a given material. Unit: metre, symbol: m.

Wavelength (noise)	The physical distance in metres between successive periodic waves (i.e. positive or negative pressure).
WBGT	**Wet Bulb Globe Temperature.**
WBV	**Whole Body Vibration**
WCI	**Wind Chill Index.**
Weils Disease	See **Leptospirosis.**
Wet Bulb Globe Temperature	One of several **heat stress indices** used to judge the severity of the thermal environment and the risk of heat casualties under physical exercise. It enables the calculation of a work/rest regime for a particular situation.
Wet Collector	**Air cleaning device** comprising a chamber packed with various substances which are wetted by a downwards stream of water. Contaminated air is introduced at the base of the chamber and forced upwards through the wet packing which collects **dust** allowing clean air to pass through the top.
Wet Scrubber	Form of **wet collector** in which contaminated air is passed through a curtain of water. Suitable for removal of medium to coarse particles.
Whistle Blower	A euphemism for a person who makes a **qualifying disclosure** under the Public Interest Disclosure Act.
White Paper	A statement of the Government's policy on a particular issue circulated in Parliament as a basis for discussion and debate.
WHO	**World Health Organisation.**
Whole Body Vibration	Especially associated with lumbar pain and spinal damage but includes ill-health effects such as nausea, unbalance and blurred vision. Normally caused while driving vehicles such as dumpers, tractors and lift trucks or working near large machinery.
Wind Chill Index	One of several **heat stress indices** devised specifically to assess the risks from cold. It uses the combined effect of air temperature and air velocity to determine the heat loss from the exposed skin.

Wire Ropes	Used for **slings**, these comprise of metal strands wound tightly around strands of fibre included in the lay. This fibre is used as a reservoir for the lubricant which prevents internal abrasion.
Woolf Report	Report of a Government inquiry which introduced new rules aimed at speeding up the process of taking a civil claim through the court. The emphasis is now placed on settling a claim before it reaches the court by introducing strict timetables, **pre-action protocols** and alternative dispute resolution.
Workplace Safety Precautions	Actions taken to reduce identified risks to an acceptable level eg guards, **PPE** and **safe systems of work**.
Work-related Upper Limb Disorder	A musculoskeletal problem affecting the upper limbs commonly associated with work activities requiring repeated manipulation or movements of the fingers hands or arms. **HSE** include **vibration** exposure as a cause of work related upper limb disorder.
World Health Organisation	A UN specialized agency for health with the objective of the attainment by all peoples of the highest possible level of health. Health is defined as a state of complete physical, mental and social well-being and not merely the absence of disease or infirmity. WHO is governed by 192 Member States through the World Health Assembly.
Wrongful Dismissal	A **dismissal** without notice or with inadequate notice in circumstances where proper notice should have been given. The expression also covers dismissals which are in breach of agreed procedures.
WRULD	**Work-related Upper Limb Disorder.**
X-radiation	A form of **ionising radiation**, pure energy, originating from the inner electron shells of an atom and travelling at the speed of light. X-radiation has great penetrating power and can interact with the matter through which it passes.
X-ray	A discrete quantity of electromagnetic energy without mass or charge emitted by an X-ray machine.

X-ray Diffraction

The technique of studying the atomic and molecular structure of crystalline substances by directing **X-rays** at them. As the **X-rays** pass through the crystals they are diffracted around the atoms. The size and shape of the atoms in the crystal can be determined by measuring the position and intensity of the diffracted rays.

X-ray Fluorescence Spectrometry

A chemical analysis technique which uses an **X-ray** source to excite secondary (fluorescent) **X-rays** from the elements in the sample. The energy produced is dependant upon the electronic configuration of the atom and consequently each element will emit a characteristic **X-ray** spectrum. The intensity of selected emission lines from the spectrum can be related to the concentration of the element in the sample.

Zoonose

Any infectious diseases that can be transmitted to human beings from other vertebrate animals. The micro-organism causing the disease does not necessarily affect its animal host. Plural - zoonoses.

Case list

Useful Civil Law Cases

Duty of Care
Bourhill v Young
Brice v Brown
British Railways Board v Herrington*
Uddin v Associated Portland Cement*
Donoghue v Stevenson*

Duty to Individual
Paris v Stepney Borough Council*
Walker v Northumberland County Council*

Reasonable Foresight
Doughty v Turner
Smith v Leech Brain
Rowark v NCB

Reasonable Alternative
Hawes v Railway Executive
Bolton v Stone
Bux v Slough Metals
Qualcast v Haynes*

Safe System of Work
General Cleaning Contractors v Christmas*
Speed v Swift (Thomas) & Co Ltd*

Safe Place of Work
Latimer v AEC*
Paine v Colne Valley Electricity Supply Company*

Negligence not cause of Injury
McWilliams v Sir William Arrol*

Novus Actus Interveniens
Scott v Sheppard

Date of Knowledge
Thompson v Smith Ship Repairers*

Proper Equipment
Bradford v Robinson Rentals*
Davey v New Merton Board Mills Limited*
Knowles v Liverpool County Council*
Machray v Stewart and Lloyd Ltd*

Liability for the torts of independent contractors
Ellis v Sheffield Gas Consumer's Co
Tarry v Ashton
Honeywill & Stein v Larkin Bros
Rylands v Fletcher*

Res Ipsa Loquitur
Byrne v Boadle
Scott v London St Katherine's Docks

Volenti Non Fit Injuria
Hall v Brooklands Auto
Bowater v Rowley Regis
Baker v Hopkins*
Smith v Baker & Sons*
ICI v Shatwell*

Contributory Negligence
Sayers v Harlow UDC
Uddin v Associated Portland Cement*
Bux v Slough Metals

Vicarious Liability
Lister v Romford Ice and Cold Storage Co Ltd*
Lindsay v Connell
Mersey Docks and Harbour Board v Coggins and Griffiths Ltd*
Rose v Plenty *

Competent Staff
Hudson v Ridge Manufacturing Co Ltd*

Reasonably Practicable
Edwards v NCB*
Marshall v Gotham*

Practicable
Adsett v K & L Steelfounders & Engineers *

Employer's Duty
Wilsons & Clyde Coal v English*

Employee
Ferguson v Dawson and Partners Ltd*

Properly Maintained Equipment
Barkway v South Wales Transport*

Breach of Statute (absolute)
John Summers and Sons v Frost*
Corn v Weir's Glass (Hanley) Ltd*

Retrospective Liability
Cambridge Water Co v Eastern Counties Leather plc*

These cases, in alphabetical order, illustrate the principles of civil actions.
* indicates cases specified by the NEBOSH Syllabus

Adsett v K & L Steelfounders & Engineers (1953)

Adsett contracted pneumoconiosis from silica dust while working in a foundry. The employer installed a dust extractor as soon as they thought of the idea but this was well after the onset of Adsett's disease. The case was brought on the basis of s47 of the Factories Act 1937 which required the employer to take all practicable measures to protect employees from the inhalation of dust.

The case failed on the principle that no measure could be 'practicable' if it was not within current knowledge and invention. The employers had not breached their statutory duty. Adsett appealed arguing that the technology existed but that his employers had not thought of this particular application for it. The Court of Appeal upheld the decision of the lower court, stating that for a measure to be practicable it had to be known for its application by people in the industry and especially by experts.

Baker v Hopkins & Son Ltd (1959)

Two men descended a well to repair a petrol pump and were overcome and collapsed. A doctor went to their assistance and was also overcome and died. It was held that the defendant was negligent. The volenti defence fails because of the moral duty to rescue protect life and prevent injury.

Barkway v South Wales Transport (1950)

A lorry ran out of control when its brake pipe burst and killed a postman on the pavement. His widow sued the lorry operator. The circumstances of the brake failure were most unusual, due to severe corrosion which gave no advance warning of failure. In defence the employer could show no evidence of a system of regular and thorough inspections but said that only 60% of the pipe was easily visible and that it was not recommended that brake pipes be removed for inspection.

It was held that the employer must produce evidence showing what steps were taken for inspection and maintenance to keep equipment in good order. They had failed to do this and were liable in negligence.

Bolton v Stone (1951)

A cricket club had played for about 90 years on their ground and no ball had ever struck anyone on the highways near the ground although a few had been hit out by exceptional players in their history. One day, however, the unfortunate Miss Stone was hit by a ball, driven out of the ground by a visiting batsman. At the time she was standing in the road outside her house.

The House of Lords decided that since the chance of such an accident happening was small, no reasonable person on the cricket club's committee would have taken precautions such as raising the height of the perimeter fence, which was 17 feet high. The claim based on negligence therefore failed. The result of the opinions of their Lordships is that there is no duty to take precautions against a danger which is no more than a remote possibility. It must first be shown that an accident is likely to happen, and secondly, that if it does happen, it is likely to cause injury. In this case the cricket club had taken reasonable care - the increasing of the perimeter fence height being unreasonable.

Bourhill (or Hay) v Young (1943)

Young was a motor-cyclist who was killed in a collision with a car as a result of his careless driving. The plaintiff heard the collision from a distance, and upon approaching the scene she saw some blood in the road. This caused her to suffer nervous shock and later she gave birth to a stillborn child.

Bourhill sued Young's representatives, but it was held that her action must fail. Although Young might have been expected to have foreseen injury to a person in the immediate vicinity of the accident, he could not reasonably be expected to foresee injury to a person so far from the spot as the plaintiff had been at the time of the collision.

Bowater v Rowley Regis Corporation (1944)

The plaintiff (employee of R.R.C) was asked to take out an unruly horse and cart. The plaintiff protested but the foreman insisted. The horse bolted and injured the plaintiff. R.R.C were held to be negligent in supplying dangerous plant. Their defence of volenti failed, L.J Scott said "man cannot be said to be truly willing unless he is in a position to choose freely. Free choice requires (a) knowledge of the danger, and (b) the absence in his mind of any feeling of constraint". Hence, compliance with employer's request is not normally consent.

Bradford v Robinson Rentals (1967)

A service engineer was sent on a 450 mile trip to pick up a new van. Neither vehicle had a heater and because of the exceptionally cold weather he was affected by frostbite. He had raised the probability of inclement weather before the trip after hearing adverse weather reports and warning from the AA not to make unnecessary journeys.

It was held that although frostbite was unforeseeable in England, some degree of injury was foreseeable due to the extreme cold. The employer should not have sent him on the journey or made sure he was protected against the cold.

Brice v Brown (1984)

A mother was alarmed by injuries to her daughter when both were passengers in a taxi involved in a collision caused by the negligence of the defendant. It was held that the defendant was liable in negligence for the mother's resulting mental illness.

British Railways Board v Herrington (1972)

An electrified railway line owned by BRB ran through property open to the public, the fences on either side of the track were in poor repair and in April 1965 children were seen on the line. A particular place in the fence had been used as a route to cross the railway. In June 1965 the plaintiff, a child of six, was severely injured when he stepped on the line, having passed through the broken fence. The plaintiff claimed damages for negligence on the part of BRB due to the disrepair of the fence through which he had passed.

The House of Lords held that whilst occupiers do not owe the same duty to trespassers which they owe to lawful visitors, they owe trespassers a duty to take such steps as common sense or 'common humanity' would dictate, to avert the danger, or warn persons coming onto the premises of its presence.

If the presence of the trespasser is known or reasonably to be anticipated by the occupier, then the occupier has a duty to the trespasser, but it is a lower and less onerous duty than the one which the occupier owes to a lawful visitor.

NOTE; this case is now supported by the Occupier's Liability Act 1984

Bux v Slough Metals Ltd [1974]

Mr Bux was injured when molten metal splashed up from a ladle he was carrying to a casting mould. He was not wearing goggles.

Goggles had been bought for the workforce and an effort had been made to persuade the men to wear them. However, due to the fact that the goggles steamed up every twenty minutes or so, the practice of wearing goggles had lapsed. It was found as a fact by the trial judge that Mr Bux would have worn goggles if the management had persisted in their efforts to persuade the men to take to the goggles. Mr Bux claimed damages for the company's failure to make more strenuous efforts to enforce the use of goggles. His claim succeeded in the High Court and his employers appealed.

It was held by the Court of Appeal that the question of whether, having provided a safety device, the employer is under an obligation to enforce its use is dependant on the facts of each case. No firm rule can be laid down. But a very important factor to consider is the risk of serious injury to the employee. And less experienced employees are often under greater risk then experienced ones.

Byrne v Boadle (1863)

A barrel of flour fell from a teagle opening and injured a passerby. It was held **Res Ipsa Loquitur.** - barrels properly handled do not generally so fall and negligence may be inferred.

Cambridge Water Co v Eastern Counties Leather plc (1994)

Eastern Counties Leather were using a substance called perchloroethane (PCE). In decanting this substance, some spilled on the ground from time to time, but PCE evaporates rapidly in the air, and no special precautions were taken. Twenty years later, Cambridge Water Co found that PCE had entered one of their boreholes 1 1/4 miles away, polluting the water they extracted from it. The specialists they engaged were able to show that the PCE in the borehole had come from ECL's site. The case went to the House of Lords, who ruled in favour of ECL, and CWC's claim for £2 million was rejected. There are a number of significant points:

1. Although ECL's foreman must have known of the spillages, it was unreasonable for him to foresee that the PCE might turn up twenty years later in a borehole 1 ¼ miles away, having travelled by a fairly complex route through the underlying strata.
2. In an issue like this, where, under the tort of nuisance, there is strict liability, the rules should be made by Parliament, not by the Courts.
3. By the time the problem became apparent, the pollutant had long since passed beyond ECL's controls, and nothing could be done about it.
4. The fact that it was possible to trace the PCE back to ECL shows that it is increasingly possible to trace pollution back to its source - polluter beware!

Corn v Weir's Glass (Hanley) Ltd (1960)

The bottom flight of stairs of a building that was being erected had no hand-rail and was only partially completed. The plaintiff, a glazier employed by the defendants, was descending the flight of stairs carrying a sheet of glass in the crook of his right arm whilst steadying the pane with his left hand above his head. A gust of wind caused the plaintiff to overbalance leading him to fall a distance of two or three feet and suffer consequent injury.

The Building (Safety, Health and Welfare) Regulations 1948 reg. 27(1) stated: 'stairs shall be provided...with hand-rails or other efficient means to prevent the fall of persons except for the time and to the extent necessary for the access of persons or the movement of materials'. Reg. 27(2) defines a hand-rail as: 'something whose function is to be gripped and thus make a fall less likely'. This is distinct from the definition of a guard-rail which is defined as: 'something whose function is to provide a barrier and prevent a fall'.

As the defendants could not show that the absence of the hand-rail was reasonably necessary as a practical matter to allow materials to be carried up the stairs it was held that the defendants were in breach of their statutory duty under reg. 27(1). However, the defendants were not found liable for the injury because the plaintiff had not established that the presence of the hand-rail would have protected him from injury, as he had no hand free when he fell. Moreover, had a hand-rail been provided, it need not have been of sufficient strength to bar his fall (i.e. it is not a 'guard-rail'). The plaintiff's injury was therefore not caused by the defendants' breach of statutory duty.

Davie v New Merton Board Mills Limited (1958)

Davie was injured when a defective chisel shattered but his claim failed when the employer showed that the equipment had been bought from a reputable supplier and that the injury was caused by a hidden defect over which they had no reasonable control. This was sufficient to discharge their duty.

This decision has since been overruled by **statute law** in the form of the **Employers' Liability (Defective Equipment) Act 1969** which allows an injured employee to claim from the employer in the first instance because of some defect in the materials, equipment or plant.

Donoghue v Stevenson (1932)

A man bought from a retailer a bottle of ginger-beer manufactured by the defendant. The man gave the bottle to his lady friend who became ill from drinking the contents. The bottle contained the decomposed remains of a snail. The bottle was opaque so that the noxious substance could not have been seen and was not discovered until the lady was refilling her glass. The consumer sued the manufacturer in negligence. Held (by the house of Lords) that the manufacturer was liable to the consumer in negligence.

Doughty v Turner Manufacturing Co Ltd (1964)

A fellow employee of Doughty let an asbestos cement cover fall into a cauldron of molten metal which resulted in an explosion that injured Doughty. At the time it was unknown that asbestos cement, coming into contact with molten metal, would result in an explosion. No similar accidents of this type had been known previously.

It was held that the accident was not reasonably foreseeable, although the action of the defendant's servant was the direct cause of the accident. The defendant was held, therefore, not to be liable.

Edwards v NCB (1949)

The degree of care, the amount of effort required and the money needed to be expended by the employer will depend chiefly on the magnitude of the risk.

In Edwards v N.C.B (1949) L.J Asquith said, 'a computation must be made in which the quantum of risk is placed on one scale, and the sacrifice involved in the measures necessary for averting the risk is placed in the other'. At one end of the scale there is only a remote possibility of injury, whereupon no precautions at all will need to be taken (though risk ought not to be disregarded unless it is extremely small). At the other end of the scale, an exacting standard of care is required of manufacturers, of say, explosives and persons engaged in ultra-hazardous activities.

The magnitude of the risk depends partly on the probability of an accident occurring but partly also on the gravity of the results if it does occur.

Ellis v Sheffield Gas Consumer's Co (1853)

The gas company employed a contractor to dig up streets although they had no authority to do so. The plaintiff fell over a pile of stone left by the contractor and sued the defendants who were held liable for the unlawful act. Where a contract is placed which causes the contractor to commit a tort, for example, asking a contractor to enter someone else's premises (trespass), or to create a nuisance, the client will have strict liability.

Fairchild and Others v Glenhaven Funeral Services and Others (2002)

In December 2001, the Court of Appeal gave judgment in the cases of Mrs Fairchild and Mrs Fox, widows of mesothelioma victims, and of Mr Matthews, who was dying of mesothelioma. The Court held that, where a mesothelioma sufferer had worked with asbestos for two or more employers, he or his widow were unable to recover damages because they could not show in which employment the fatal fibre(s) had been inhaled.

The decision was appealed and five Law Lords unanimously decided that all three appeals succeeded in full.

Their Lordships considered that the balance of justice in such cases lay overwhelmingly on the side of the injured victims, holding that each defendant who had significantly exposed a sufferer to asbestos was liable to pay the entirety of the damages. Where there are two or more defendants that are sued, they will share the damages between them. Where only one significant asbestos employer can be sued, because the others are insolvent and uninsured, that defendant must pay the whole value of the claim.

Ferguson v Dawson and Partners Ltd (1976)

Ferguson, a self-employed builder, fell from a roof and sued Dawson for failing to provide a safe place of work. Their defence was that the duty only applied to employees of the company and therefore Ferguson was not entitled to claim.

The court ruled that under the way the industry operated at the time, employing labour casually from day to day, providing tools and equipment, and hiring and firing as though they were employed it was contrary to the facts to call them sub-contractors. To all intents and purposes they may as well be employees.

General Cleaning Contractors Ltd v Christmas (1952)

Christmas, who was employed by the company, was a very experienced window cleaner. The company made safety belts available but Christmas, who was cleaning windows at the Caledonian Club in London, was not using a safety belt because there were no fittings on the building to which such a belt could have been attached. Christmas, who was obtaining hand and foot holds from the window frames and sills, fell and was injured when a defective sash dropped on to his hand causing him to lose his hold.

It was held by the House of Lords that the company was liable. It should have provided wedges to prevent sashes from falling and instructed its employees to test for dangerous sashes. There was a breach of the duty to provide a safe system of work. In planning such a system the company should have taken into account the fact that its employees might take the risk of working without the safety belts. The Caledonian Club were not liable as occupiers because they could expect an experienced window cleaner to take account of the possibility of defective sashes and make provision for his own safety.

Hall v Brooklands Auto Racing Club (1933)

Hall paid for admission to watch car races. A car shot over the railings and killed two spectators. The court found that the precautions taken were adequate and held that Hall had consented to accept the risks normally inherent in motor sports, defence of **Volenti Non Fit Injuria** applies .

Hawes v Railway Executive (1952)

A railway ganger doing minor running repairs to a stretch of electrified railway line slipped, and was killed on the live rail. His widow claimed damages against her husband's employer. The widow was able to prove that his death was likely; all he had to do was to put one foot wrong. The risk was well known to the employer, as also, of course, to the employee. The widow also showed that a foolproof way of preventing the accident would have been turning off the electrical power whilst men were at work on the line.

However, turning off the electricity to the track would have meant many miles of track would have been unusable. It was clearly impractical to do this every time minor repair work was necessary. Such rail traffic disruption that would result from switching off the power would clearly not have been tolerated by society as users of the rail services. The widow's claim was rejected as it was unreasonable to take the precautions outlined, hence negligence was not shown.

Honeywill & Stein v Larkin Bros (1934)

The defendants were independent contractors engaged by H&S to take flash pictures of the interior of a cinema. The magnesium powder flash set fire to the cinema and caused damage. The cinema owners claimed damages from the plaintiffs who in turn were granted an indemnity from the photographers. Liability exists where an independent contractor is engaged to carry out 'extra-hazardous' activity.

Hudson v Ridge Manufacturing Co Ltd (1957)

Hudson was injured when a fellow employee known for playing practical jokes caused him to fall and break his wrist. The judges ruled that it was the employer's duty to reprimand, discipline or dismiss if necessary to remove this danger.

ICI v Shatwell (1965)

Two certified shotblasters, about to set an explosion, found that the wire available was too short to extend to a position of safety. They sent another employee to get more wire but proceeded to start testing the circuitry whilst standing in the open. An explosion occurred injuring both men and each sued the employer for vicarious liability of each towards the other.

In their defence ICI said that each employee had voluntarily accepted the risk of each other's negligence by conspiring to contravene regulations and duties that they knew only too well. The defence succeeded but with a proviso that if one employee had seniority over another it would not apply and would equally not be available to an employer who was directly in breach of their common law obligations.

Knowles v Liverpool County Council (1992)

Knowles was injured when a flagstone he was handling broke. His claim was founded upon The Employer's Liability (Defective Equipment) Act 1969 arguing that the flagstone fell into the category of work equipment and he succeeded.

On appeal to the House of Lords their lordships agreed that the wording of the Act should be construed widely enough to embrace every article of whatever kind provided by the employer.

John Summers & Sons Ltd v Frost, (1955)

The respondent was employed by the appellants at their steelworks as a maintenance fitter. Whilst grinding a piece of metal on a power-driven grinding machine he was injured when his thumb came into contact with the revolving grindstone. The only part of the revolving grindstone exposed was an arc about 7in long, there being a gap of ³/₈ inch between the hood and the revolving arc of stone.

It was held by the House of Lords that since the grinding stone was a dangerous part of machinery within Sect. 14(1), Factories Act , there was an absolute obligation under that sub-section that the grinding stone should be securely fenced to prevent such injury as is reasonably foreseeable, regardless of whether the workman using the machine is careless or inattentive. This machine therefore, was not securely fenced and the appellants were in breach of their duty so to do, although the consequences of securely fencing the grinding machine would be to render it commercially unusable.

Latimer v A.E.C. Ltd., (1953)

The appellant was a milling machine operator employed by the respondents. Some 4,000 persons were employed at the works which were about 15 acres in extent. Owing to an exceptionally heavy rainstorm the factory became flooded and the flood water mixed with an oil liquid used for cooling on the machines. After the water had drained away an oily slippery film was left on the floor surface. The respondents spread sawdust on the floor, but owing to the very large area and unprecedented flood there was insufficient sawdust to cover the whole floor. The appellant slipped on the part of the floor which was not treated and was injured.

It was held by the House of Lords that the respondents had taken every reasonable step to obviate danger to the appellant; they were not liable for negligence at common law. The fact that the accident would not have occurred had the defendant closed the workshops and sent everyone home was relevant, but this would have caused great economic loss which could not reasonably have been demanded. The judges recognised that in circumstances of extreme danger it would be reasonable to expect part or all of a factory to be closed, but the only risk in this case was one of slipping.

Lindsay v Connell (1951)

An employee doing his normal job negligently hit Lindsay's finger. The employer was held vicariously liable for the employee's negligence.

Lister v Romford Ice and Cold storage Co. Ltd., (1957)

The defendants' lorry driver negligently reversed the company's vehicle into another servant of the company (his father) who received damages from the company under the doctrine of vicarious liability. The defendants were insured against this liability and the insurance company paid the damages and, under the doctrine of subrogation, sued the lorry driver in the name of the company to recover what they had paid. This was held unanimously by the House of Lords that the lorry driver, as a servant of the company, owed them a duty to perform his work with reasonable care and skill, and that a servant who involves his master in vicarious liability by reason of negligence is liable in damages to the master for breach of contract. The damages will in such a case amount to a complete indemnity in respect of the amount which the employer has been held vicariously liable to pay the injured plaintiff.

Machray v Stewart and Lloyd Ltd (1964)

Machray was an experienced rigger who was asked to raise some piping to a point 70 feet above the ground. In the absence of a crane he proposed to use a chain block and tackle but none was available.

Under pressure from the supervisor he used a rope block and tackle instead and during the lift the piping swung out of control hitting him in the process. His claim that the company had failed to provide equipment that was suitable for the job was accepted by the court who also rejected completely a notion of contributory negligence because of the pressure placed on him by the supervisor.

Marshall v Gotham Co Ltd (1954)

Regulations required the roof of a mine to be made secure so far as reasonably practicable. The usual practice in a gypsum mine is to test the roof with a hammer and bring down unsafe portions of the roof, as distinct from the practice in coal mines of having systematic support by means of props. The roof of a mine had been tested in this way, but collapsed owing to a rare geological fault which had not been known to occur in the mine for twenty years.   Further, systematic support would not have prevented the fall though it might have minimised it. The House of Lords held that it was the known risk which had to be taken into account, and balanced against safety measures, and that in the circumstances the defence was established,

Lord Reid said "...if a precaution is practicable it must be taken unless in the whole circumstances that would be unreasonable. And as men's lives may be at stake it should not lightly be held that to take a practicable precaution is unreasonable.....The danger was a very rare one. The trouble and expense involved in the use of the precautions, while not prohibitive, would have been considerable. The precautions would not have afforded anything like complete protection against the danger, and their adoption would have had the disadvantage of giving false sense of security".

Mersey Docks and Harbour Board v Coggins and Griffiths Ltd (1946)

The defendants hired a crane and an operator from Mersey Docks under a contract which stated that the crane operator was to be regarded as an employee of the defendant. The crane operator negligently injured another of Coggins & Griffith's employees and the question arose as to which "employer" was liable for his actions. It was held that liability was not to be determined solely by the wording of the contract between the parties. Mersey Docks was the employer of the operator and would remain liable unless they could show that full control over the crane operator had passed to the defendant. They had failed to establish this. The employer is the person who can hire and fire, pays the wages, pays the national insurance etc. and is identified as such in the contract of employment.

McWilliams (or Cummings) v Sir William Arrol & Co (1962)

A steel erector fell seventy feet and was killed. Evidence showed that the use of a safety belt would have prevented the fall but that it would not have been worn if provided. It was held by the House of Lords that failure to provide equipment was not the cause of damage.

Paine v Colne Valley Electricity Supply Company (1938)

Paine was electrocuted when working in an electrical kiosk which had been set up by a skilled contractor who failed to install proper insulation. It was held that the employer had failed to fulfill their duty of care to provide a safe place of work, a responsibility that could not be delegated however competent the contractors.

Paris v Stepney Borough Council (1951)

The plaintiff was employed by the defendants on vehicle maintenance. He had the use of only one eye and the defendants were aware of this. The plaintiff was endeavouring to remove a bolt from the chassis of a vehicle, and was using a hammer for the purpose, when a chip of metal flew into his good eye so that he became totally blind. The plaintiff claimed damages from his employers for negligence in that he had not been supplied with goggles. The defendants showed in evidence that it was not the usual practice in trades of this nature to supply goggles, at least where the employees were men with two good eyes. The House of Lords held that the gravity of the harm likely to be caused would influence a reasonable employer, so that the duty of care to a one-eyed employee required the supply of goggles, and Paris therefore succeeded.

Qualcast (Wolverhampton) Ltd v Haynes (1959)

Mr Haynes worked in a foundry where his job was to pour molten metal from a hand-held ladle into a mould. On one occasion the ladle slipped and some of the molten metal splashed onto his boot. He was not wearing special protective leather spats or heavy boots. Either of these would have protected his foot. Instead he had chosen to wear a normal pair of working boots. The molten metal penetrated the boot and injured his foot.

Protective spats were available at no charge from the stores. This was well known and some of the men wore spats as a matter of course. Heavy boots were available, but these had to be paid for. Mr Haynes claimed damages. He alleged that the employers should have enforced the use of spats and not just left it to the men to ask for them if they wanted.

It was held by the House of Lords (Lord Cohen dissenting) that a failure of duty on the part of the appellants, as employers of Haynes, had not been established. Haynes was an experienced moulder and by making protective clothing available to him they had fulfilled their duty to take reasonable care for his safety, despite the fact that they had not brought pressure to bear upon him to wear the spats. The employers therefore had not been in breach of duty.

Rose v Plenty (1976)

A milk float driver who knew he was not allowed to have children help him with his round employed a thirteen year old boy, who was subsequently injured due to the milkman's negligence. The dairy argued that the milkman was acting outside the course of his employment so that they were not liable for the boy's injuries. The court held the dairy to be vicariously liable. The milkman was engaged in his employment and the accident occurred within the scope of it even though he was breaking the rules at the time.

Rowark v National Coal Board (1986)

Mr Rowark was a miner. Part of his work involved hauling half-ton wagons of waste material along a 400-yard stretch of rail track over a three month period. He developed tenosynovitis (a painful inflammation of the wrist tendons). He claimed damages. The employers defence was that this specific condition could not have been foreseen as a consequence of this kind of work.

So long as the general type of injury was reasonably foreseeable, a claim for damages could be made out. It was not necessary for the specific type of injury to be foreseen. In this case, some kind of strain to the wrists was foreseeable to a person expected to push such heavy loads over such a prolonged period It was held that there was a breach of duty in failing to provide a powered haulage system.

Rylands v Fletcher (1868)

The defendant engaged independent contractors to construct a reservoir on his land. The contractors came across a disused mineshaft which they filled in, not knowing that it was connected to the plaintiff's mines. When the reservoir filled the water escaped and flooded the plaintiff's mine. This brings about a strict liability regardless of intent or negligence. "A person who for his own purposes brings onto his land and collects and keeps there anything likely to do mischief if it escapes, must keep it in at his peril, and if he does not do so, is answerable for all the damage which is a natural consequences of its escape".

The implications are clear, and there are few defences, which are:

- The escape was the plaintiff's fault.
- The escape was an Act of God (hard to prove).
- The escape was due to the wrongful act of a stranger.
- The damage was caused by works done for the common benefit of both parties.
- There was some statutory authority for the defendants to do what they did.

Sayers v Harlow U.D.C (1958)

The plaintiff entered a public toilet owned by Harlow Urban District Council. Owing to a defective lock she could not get out and she attempted to climb out. She fell and was injured. The defendants were negligent and Sayers contributed to this negligence by trying to balance on revolving object (toilet roll holder) to climb out. Her contribution was assessed at 25%.

Scott v London St Katherines Docks (1865)

As a Customs officer passed a warehouse, 6 bags of sugar fell on him. It was held that **RES IPSA LOQUITUR** applied here and negligence may be inferred. Bags of Sugar do not fall of their own accord.

Scott v Sheppard (1773)

On Fair day, the defendant threw a lighted squib on a market stall which was then thrown from stall to stall, eventually hitting the plaintiff in eye causing loss of the eye. It was held that there was no break in the chain of causation, the consequence was direct, there was no *Novus Actus Interveniens:* the defendant should have anticipated the result of his actions.

Smith v Baker and Sons (1891)

Smith was working in a railway siding while heavy rocks were being lifted overhead. He complained and after being invited to leave he decided to remain at work. His employers claimed that he knew of the risk and willing placed himself in it. The notion was rejected by the House of Lords who said that remaining at work did not amount to consenting to the risk.

Smith v Crossley Brothers (1951)

Smith was injured when two fellow apprentices, in an act of extreme horseplay, injected compressed air into his body. The Court of Appeal held that such an action could not reasonably have been foreseen by the employer. The apprentices were not carrying out authorised duties in an unauthorised manner, but were engaged in an act which was not part of their work at all. They were off on a frolic of their own and the employers could not be held responsible.

Smith v Leech Braine & Co Ltd (1962)

Some molten zinc flew out of a galvanising tank causing a burn to the lip of an employee. Cancer eventually developed on the site of the burn, which lead to the man's death after three years. The widow sued her husband's employer. It was held that the defendants were liable, although the man's death was clearly not a foreseeable result of the accident.

N.B The main difference between this and the Doughty case is an unforeseeable cause of accident in the Doughty case, and an unforeseeable resulting injury in this case. The cause of the accident in Smith v Leech Braine & Co Ltd was foreseeable, and hence the employer was negligent.

Speed v Swift (Thomas) & Co Ltd (1943)

Speed was injured when a winch on board ship caught on the perimeter railing of his ship. The railing broke and fell on him in a barge below. The winch was known to be unsafe and the railing known to be already broken and therefore likely to become dislodged if hit. It was held that the employer was negligent and should have ensured that the fencing was protected in some way so as to avoid hooks becoming caught up.

Lord Greene said "I do not venture to suggest a definition of what is meant by a system. But it may include the physical layout of the job, the setting of the stage, the sequence in which the work has to be carried out, the provision of warnings and notices, and the issue of special instructions............ a system may have to be modified or improved to meet circumstances which may arise; such modifications or improvements appear to me to fall equally under the heading of system".

Sutherland v Hatton and others (2002)

2002 Four notable cases went to the Court of Appeal
- Sutherland v Hatton
- Somerset County Council v Barber
- Baker Refractories v Bishop
- Sandwell Metropolitan Borough Council v Jones

1   Hatton, a secondary school teacher, was awarded £90K damages after suffering a nervous breakdown. The School's appeal was upheld by the court on the grounds that Hatton gave her employer no notice that her workload was too great. Her personal circumstances had created a number of stressful life events which led to absenteeism which, the court held, would be reasonable for her employer to attribute to those events. She made no complaint about her workload and there was no sufficiently clear indication that she was likely to suffer psychiatric injury.

2   Barber, another secondary school teacher, was awarded £101K damages after taking early retirement because of depressive symptoms caused by reorganisation at school. The workload of other teachers was compared with his and the court decided he was no worse off. Nor did he tell his employer of his symptoms.

It was held that there was no point at which the employer could reasonably have taken positive steps to help him.

3   Bishop suffered a mental breakdown and tried to commit suicide. His original claim brought £7K damages pending further review of financial losses.

The Appeal Court revoked this, stating that others (colleagues) seemed quite able to cope with the restructuring that had caused him his distress. When off work with anxiety, he did not tell his employers the reason and did not report that his GP had advised him to change his job.

The Court accepted that whilst his employer knew that he was unhappy, it could not reinvent his old job.

4   Jones developed anxiety and depression after a period of extreme work and was awarded £157K damages.

She had complained about her excessive workload but no help had been forthcoming. Her award was allowed by the Court on the basis that the employer knew of her excessive workload and that it was reasonable that they should have foreseen that harm could result from this stress.

The Court of Appeal went on to lay down some general guidelines on how stress claims should be dealt with by the courts. Case two above was overturned on appeal to the House of Lords but they unanimously agreed with the Appeal Court's guidelines.

Tarry v Ashton (1876)

Ashton engaged a contractor to inspect and renew a heavy lamp on the front of the premises. The lamp was negligently repaired and later collapsed and injured the plaintiff. Ashton was held to be negligent and failed to discharge his duty to maintain the lamp. Liability exists for any operations on, or adjoining the highway (other than normal use).

Thompson and Others v Smiths Ship-repairers (North Shields) Ltd (1984)

Thompson and five others sued for loss of hearing caused by their exposure to noise in the workplace. Thompson had been employed from 1936 to 1983 and used a pneumatic scaling tool for 25% of his work time. Tests in 1983 showed a 50% hearing loss and he wore a hearing aid at all times.

The shipbuilders were aware of the possible damage to hearing caused by the excessive noise, but there was no easy or obvious remedy. At what stage ought they to have become aware that ear-muffs of a satisfactory design were available? It was said that in the flood of printed material employers cannot be expected to see every small item, but a stage was reached when references to protective devices were common and they should have known about them, and in any case there were organisations available to give advice.

The question to be answered was this: `From what date would a reasonable employer, with proper but not extraordinary solicitude for the welfare of his workers, have identified the problem of excessive noise in his yard, recognised that it was capable of solution, weighed up the potential advantages and disadvantages of that solution, decided to adopt it, acquired a supply of the protectors, set in train the programme of education necessary to persuade the men and their representatives that the system was useful and not potentially deleterious, experimented with the system, and finally put it into full effect?' The leaflet "Noise and the Worker" was published in 1963 and it is from this time that all employers could reasonably be expected to know of the dangers of noise.

Evidence shows that the greatest loss to hearing occurs in the early years, perhaps the first 3 - 6 years, and the judge ruled in this case that the employer could only be held liable for that loss which arose after 1963. As most of the physical injury occurred before this time, awards of damages were low.

Uddin v Associated Portland Cement Manufacturers Ltd (1965)

The plaintiff, was employed as a machine minder by the defendants in their cement factory at Dunstable. On 20th April, 1961, in an endeavour to catch a pigeon, he leaned across a revolving shaft in a place in which he was not authorised to be, and lost an arm as a result. The shaft was part of a dust extracting plant and the plaintiff's duties were solely concerned with the cement packing plant. He brought an action for damages, alleging that the shaft was a dangerous part of machinery which was required to be fenced by virtue of sect. 14(1) of the Factories Act. It was held by the Court of Appeal that the defendants were in breach of their obligation under this section, and that the plaintiff, who at the time of injury was doing an act wholly outside the scope of his employment, for his own benefit, at a place to which he knew he was not authorised to go, was not entirely debarred from recovering damages. The responsibility therefore would be apportioned on the basis of 20 percent to the defendants and 80 per cent to the plaintiff.

Walker v Northumberland County Council (1995)

A social worker of 17 years standing suffered a nervous breakdown because of overwork as a result of an increasing workload. On his return to work, he told his employers that his pressure of work must be relieved. This never happened and Walker suffered a second breakdown which resulted in him being dismissed due to ill-health.

His claim succeeded. His employer was well aware of the extreme pressure he was under. After the first breakdown they should have appreciated that he was distinctly more vulnerable to psychiatric damage and should have been provided with additional assistance. In not doing so the employer was negligent.

Wilson v Clyde Coal Co v English (1938)

The House of Lords held that "the personal duty of the employer to take reasonable care for the safety of his workmen" was threefold:

- It requires him to provide safe plant and machinery.
- To ensure he employs competent staff.
- To provide safe systems of work.

In this case, a miner was leaving the pit when the haulage plant was put into operation. He was crushed against a wall before he had time to reach a refuge hole. It was held to be an unsafe system for the haulage plant to be operated while the morning shift was leaving work.

Useful Criminal Law Cases

Extent of action to protect employees
R v Swan Hunter Shipbuilders Ltd and
Another*

Senior Manager Liability
Armour v Skeen*
R v Boal

Undertaking
R v Associated Octel Co Ltd*
R v Nelson Group Services
(Maintenance) Ltd*
R v British Steel*

Armour v Skeen (1997)

John Armour the Director of Roads for Strathclyde Regional Council was instructed under the terms of the Council's safety policy to draw up a policy statement for his directorate which he failed to do. Some time later an employee fell from a bridge and was killed. Armour was charged with neglect under section 37 of the HSW Act for his failure to follow up the instruction.

R v Associated Octel Co Ltd (1996)

Octel contracted RGP to repair the lining of a process tank. An RGP employee was injured when his lamp broke and ignited acetone vapour. The House of Lords supported the original conviction (s3 of HSW Act) as Octel's undertaking included maintenance and repair of process plant, and this undertaking put at risk a non-employee. Lord Hoffman suggested that an employer's undertaking includes any activity integrated with the general conduct of the employer's business. Contractors activities cannot be ignored, they must be subject to the same degree of care as is provided for employees.

Octel claimed the undertaking was that of RGP and that it was not part of their undertaking. They also referred to the common law position where an employer is not generally liable for the actions of an independent contractor. The court rejected the arguments by concluding that the HSW Act does not follow the common law position and that repair and maintenance was, for the purposes of s3 of HSW Act, part of the employer's undertaking. They convicted Octel on a breach of s3 of HSW Act.

Octel appealed. The Court of Appeal rejected Octel's arguments on the grounds that the meaning of the word *undertaking* is wide enough to cover activities carried out by independent contractors and that, if it is shown that a risk to a non-employee did exist, it was for the accused to show that all reasonably practicable steps were taken to eliminate or reduce that risk. The House of Lords also considered the case and supported the findings of the CA.

Lord Hoffman rejected the HSE view that *all* maintenance falls within the employer's undertaking. For instance, cleaning office curtains at the dry cleaners or maintaining a company car at a garage would fall outside the scope of an employer's undertaking.

R v British Steel plc (1995)

British Steel commissioned sub-contractors on a labour only basis to reposition a section of steel platform by cutting it free and moving it by crane. British Steel provided the supervision and equipment. The contractors cut the platform free without securing and it fell killing one of them. The company was convicted of an offence under s3 of HSW Act and appealed on the grounds that, at the level of the 'directing mind', the company had taken reasonably practicable precautions by delegating supervision. They asked the court to infer that the word employer should be construed in those terms.

The appeal was rejected. The criminal liability of the employer is absolute (subject to the defence of reasonably practicable) it cannot be delegated through supervision.

R v Boal (Francis) (1992)

The case was taken under s23 of the Fire Precautions Act 1971 which has almost identical wording to s37 of HSW Act. It arose after Boal who was manager of Foyle's bookshop in London was prosecuted for failing to comply with an enforcement notice issued by the Fire Authority. Boal accepted responsibility and submitted a guilty plea and was sentenced to three months in prison.

In an unusual concession (after a guilty plea) he was allowed to appeal against his conviction because of the inappropriate legal advice he was given. He was not a *manager* in the legal sense of the word and therefore could not be culpable under this section. The judge agreed saying that the construction of the section was to get at those responsible for deciding corporate policy and strategy and not to strike at 'underlings'.

R v Nelson Group Services (Maintenance) Ltd (1998)

Nelson group were charged with a number of offences under s3 of HSW Act in relation to unsafe practices of its employees working on gas appliances. They were convicted at Crown Court after the judge directed the jury on the issue of 'reasonably practicable'.

They appealed on the grounds that the negligent act of a fitter was not the employer conducting its undertaking. The negligent act did not prevent Nelson Group from showing that it had done all that was reasonably practicable to ensure that the dwelling occupants were not exposed to risk. The appeal succeeded.

R v Swan Hunter Shipbuilders (1979)

In 1976 there was a fire on board HMS Glasgow; 8 died. On the shift were about 1000 employees of Swan Hunter, Marriott's, Telemeter's and other contractors working side by side. Clearly all were at risk from the activities of others. SH and T (T pleaded guilty) were charged under s2 and s3 of HSW Act on indictment. SH case was heard before a jury and were duly convicted. SH appealed against prosecution under s2 and s3 on the grounds that s2 applied only to SH employees and s3 (1) did not contain a duty to provide information about the danger of oxygen enrichment nor a duty to instruct in precautions to ensure safe working.

Dangers of oxygen enrichment were well known in the industry and SH Training had recognised that employees did not really appreciate this - there was no smell, no noise, no discomfort and no real appreciation of the danger. SHT compiled a "blue book" of rules concerning this with a view to addressing this lack of appreciation and 14000 copies were made and distributed.

The essence of the appeal case to be decided was whether this "blue book" should have been distributed to subcontractors.

The Court of Appeal held that s3(1) is a strict and general duty as is s2(1) and, where s2(1) is "expanded" by s2(2), then a similar "expansion" may be inferred for s3(1), thus information and instruction for others may be necessary. This is a general duty whereas s3(3) provides a specific duty when prescribed information in prescribed cases is to be given to persons not involved in the undertaking.

It was also held that s(2) includes an inherent duty, in the circumstances, to inform and instruct others: "if the provision of a safe system of work for the benefit of his own employees involves information and instruction as to the potential dangers being given to persons other than the employer's own employees, then the employer is under a duty to provide such information and instruction". In the absence of such provision the system would not be a **safe** system and the employer would **not** discharge his duty under s2(1). The onus is on the defendant to show that it was not reasonably practicable in the circumstances to provide information and instruction to non-employees. The defendant had failed to do this and the appeal against conviction under s2 and s3 was rejected.

Common Occurring Substances

Appendix 2 contains brief outlines of the source, health effects and symptoms associated with some commonly occurring chemical substances. These include:

Ammonia
Asbestos
Benzene
Carbon Monoxide
Chromium Compounds
Isocyanates
Lead (Organic)
Lead (Inorganic)
Methylene-bis-o-chloraniline (MBOCA)
Silica (Silicon Dioxide)
Sodium Hydroxide (caustic soda)
Tar (Coal Tar)
Trichloroethylene (TCE)
Vinyl Chloride Monomer

Substance **Source of exposure**	**Ammonia** A strongly alkaline **irritant** gas and is used as a fertiliser, cleaning agent and refrigerant.
Route of entry	Inhalation.
Health effects - **common signs and** **symptoms**	Affects the upper respiratory tract quickly with mouth and throat pain, cough, mucous membrane swelling and ulceration. Longer exposure would lead to **pulmonary oedema** (swelling of the lung tissues, with breathlessness and sometimes "drowning"). A chronic effect can be airways obstruction. Liquid splashes will burn the skin at point of contact or the eyes causing conjunctivitis and keratitis. More serious effects include ulceration of the cornea with subsequent scar tissue and corneal opacities.
Substance **Source of exposure**	**Asbestos** Asbestos refers to a group of compound metallic silicates which have crystallized to form long thin fibres. They withstand very high temperatures and are poor heat conductors and therefore have been used in insulation materials. **Chrysotile** (white asbestos) is abundant and easily mined and makes up 90% of world production. It is used in textiles, in friction materials (like brake pads) and for reinforcing cement and plastics. Use of **Crocidolite** (blue asbestos) is prohibited in the UK because of its carcinogenic potential. **Amosite** (brown asbestos) is used in insulation.
Route of entry	By inhalation. The fibres are respirable but very difficult to clear from the lungs, especially the longer they are relative to their width.
Health effects - **common signs and** **symptoms**	The effects of asbestos are restricted to the skin, lungs and pleural and peritoneal membranes. Asbestos fibres penetrating skin set up an inflammatory reaction with hyperkeratosis to produce an asbestos wart. In the lungs inhalation of asbestos leads to a fibrotic **pneumoconiosis**. In contrast to **silicosis** the fibrosis of **asbestosis** is predominantly in the lower zones of the lungs.

Asbestosis presents with dry cough, breathlessness, weight loss, and often finger clubbing. The shadows on chest x-ray are linear initially, becoming larger and less regular as symptoms develop. Asbestos bodies (beaded rod-like bodies up to 150μ long and coated with an iron-containing protein) show up often on examination of sputum and are evidence of exposure but not of total asbestos load or of **asbestosis**.

Asbestosis alone can lead to respiratory failure and death, but death is more often related to the asbestos cancers. Heavy asbestos exposure can lead to bronchial carcinoma and this risk is potentiated by cigarette smoking. Development of finger clubbing in someone with **asbestosis** is often the first sign of malignancy.

Substance **Source of exposure**	**Benzene** Produced by distillation of coal tar, a by-product of coke production. It is used in the rubber, plastics, paint and glue industries, in closed systems wherever possible.
Route of entry	The liquid can be absorbed through the skin, or (rarely) ingested, but the most important route of entry is by inhalation of the vapour.
Health effects - common signs and symptoms	Benzene is fat soluble and remains for a long time in fat stores, especially in females. They are thus more at risk than men, but individuals of either sex can be particularly vulnerable. Benzene is mostly excreted through the lungs but the liver metabolises some to produce conjugated phenols which appear in the urine.

Acute poisoning through exposure to very high vapour concentration causes giddiness progressing to unconsciousness and death if not removed from the source. The major effect of chronic benzene exposure is poisoning of the bone marrow. Benzene can reduce platelet production (leading to clotting defects and purpura) red cell production (leading to anaemia) and white cell production (reducing the ability to fight infection). A total halt in blood synthesis can occur (aplastic anaemia) and any of these changes may happen years after exposure has ceased. Chronic benzene poisoning can also lead to impairment of balance and hearing and altered performance in behavioural tests. It can also damage heart muscle and causes rhythm abnormalities.

Benzene or a metabolite of it interfering with **DNA** synthesis may lead to opposite effects in bone marrow with overgrowth of any of the cell types and a variety of subsequent leukaemias. Alcohol consumption enhances benzene's toxic effects on bone marrow.

Substance **Source of exposure**	**Carbon monoxide** Incomplete combustion of carbon produces carbon monoxide (instead of carbon dioxide) and it is thus found around blast furnaces, mines and the exhausts of petrol and diesel engines.
Route of entry	Inhalation.
Health effects - common signs and symptoms	Its affinity for haemoglobin makes it a cumulative toxin and thus increased exertion with increased respiratory rate speeds up the onset of symptoms. It causes chemical asphyxia.

Symptoms of **hypoxia** - giddiness and headache - precede staggering and unconsciousness. The carbon monoxide is completely eliminated via the lungs after exposure and the only long-term risk of acute poisoning is permanent brain damage if **hypoxia** has continued long enough.

Substance	**Chromium compounds**
Source of exposure	Metallic chromium is used in steel production and chrome plating. Its compounds are used as pigments and tanning (leather) agents.
Route of entry	Trivalent chromium compounds are poorly absorbed and thus minimally toxic, while hexavalent compounds (chromic acid and many dichromates) are absorbed through the lungs, gut and intact skin.
Health effects - common signs and symptoms	Chromium is an essential element required for carbohydrate metabolism, much is retained in the lungs, and excretion is mostly via the kidney though some is faecal. Urinary chromium concentration indicates recent exposure but is less meaningful than functional tests on the lungs (for asthma) and scrutiny of the skin (for dermatitis and ulcers).

Chromium salts (compounds) can sensitize the skin to produce allergic contact dermatitis and some can sensitize the lungs to produce **occupational asthma**. Chromic acid mist, a hazard associated with chrome plating, can cause inflammation and ulceration of the larynx, and more often, the nose. Painless ulceration of the nasal cartilage can even lead to perforation. Punched out ulcers of the skin mainly of the hands, also occur which are not very painful and are called '**chrome holes**'. **Conjunctivitis**, ulcerated eyelids and bronchitis are all possible results of exposure. The greatest danger of chromium compounds, and thought only to be those in hexavalent form, is lung **cancer**, discovered in workers in the chrome pigment industry and chromate production.

Substance	**Isocyanates**
Source of exposure	Isocyanates are used to make rubbers, foams and adhesives. Heating them causes vaporisation although TDI (toluene di-isocyanate) is volatile at room temperature.
Route of entry	NDI (1:5 naphthalene di-isocyanate) is used as a pulverised solid and can be inhaled as dust. Spraying polyurethane lacquers and urethane foams both carry inhalation risks.
Health effects - common signs and symptoms	TDI is the most volatile and most toxic. It can cause mucous membrane irritation and dermatitis, and also a confused state after several hours of high exposure.

However, isocyanates are best known for their production of **occupational asthma**. The asthma is unrelated to atopy (a predisposition of 15-30% population to asthma, hayfever and eczema) and therefore very difficult to predict in employees.

Substance	**Lead (Inorganic)**
Source of exposure	Inorganic lead exposure can occur during lead smelting, battery manufacture, pottery glazing and demolition work (involving high temperature work on structures originally painted with lead paints).
Route of entry	Inhaled as fume (most often) or ingested via contaminated hands.
Health effects - common signs and symptoms	2% of absorbed lead is carried in the blood while the majority is pooled in the skeleton where it competes with calcium at nerve synapses and in bone, affecting nerve conduction and displacing calcium in bones. Inorganic lead interferes with enzyme systems associated with haem synthesis for red blood cells. It also causes haemolysis, lassitude, weakness, general aches and pains, metallic taste in the mouth, and nausea or vomiting.

With inorganic lead abdominal pain, colic and constipation are worse and in extreme cases there may be wrist drop due to peripheral nerve effects. Thus the effects of inorganic lead are most notable in the blood and peripheral nerves. Diagnosis of inorganic lead poisoning is made possible by the finding of anaemic blood changes and increased levels of ALA (5-amino laevulinic acid) and coproporphyrin (both precursors of haem) in the urine. The blood lead level is also raised. Nowadays the classical blue line of lead sulphide (Burtonian line) on the gums is rare. Lead exposure can still lead to a high incidence of spontaneous abortions in female workers.

Substance	**Lead (Organic)**
Source of exposure	Organic lead, as tetraethyl lead (TEL), one of the anti-knock agents in petrol, can cause poisoning through careless exposure to petrol.
Route of entry	Can be inhaled but also passes through intact skin. Only organic lead can cross the blood-brain barrier.
Health effects - common signs and symptoms	2% of absorbed lead is carried in the blood while the majority is pooled in the skeleton where it competes with calcium at nerve synapses and in bone, affecting nerve conduction and displacing calcium in bones.

Lassitude, weakness, general aches and pains, metallic taste in the mouth, and nausea or vomiting are symptomatic. Organic lead produces a toxic organic psychosis. Thus the effects of organic lead predominate in the central nervous system. Diagnosis of organic lead poisoning is confirmed by a raised urinary lead level. Nowadays the classical blue line of lead sulphide (Burtonian line) on the gums is rare. Lead exposure can still lead to a high incidence of spontaneous abortions in female workers.

Substance	**Methylene-bis-o-chloraniline (MBOCA)**
Source of exposure	Used as a curing agent in urethane foam.
Route of entry	Inhalation.
Health effects -	Like many other amines it is suspected of being
common signs and	carcinogenic and has produced lung and liver tumours
symptoms	experimentally in animals. Exposed men have developed haemorrhagic cystitis. Many amines, especially B-naphthylamine fumes inhaled by gas retort workers, have caused bladder cancer in the past and thus MBOCA and the like are either substituted or those people exposed to them are extremely closely watched.

Substance	**Silica (Silicon dioxide)**
Source of exposure	Crystalline silica is found in quartz and flint and inhalation of fresh dust in occupations like sandblasting, quarrying and the pottery industry led to silicosis.
Route of entry	By inhalation
Health effects -	**Silicosis** is a fibrotic **pneumoconiosis**. Silica sets up a
common signs and	fibrotic reaction with nodules of increasing size (1mm
symptoms	1cm) and then larger conglomerations of these. Early changes on x-ray, mostly in the upper zones of the lungs, warn of **silicosis** developing before any symptoms other than dry cough appear. Once large coalescent nodules are present and breathlessness is obvious, the disease may progress despite removal from the source of silica, the degree of breathlessness will eventually make work impossible anyway. There is a high risk of developing tuberculosis on top of the existing lung damage and many **silicosis** sufferers die of heart failure.

Substance	**Sodium Hydroxide (caustic soda)**
Source of exposure	Used extensively as a cleaning agent in food manufacturing machinery amongst others. It usually takes the form of solid pellets or beads which are then mixed with water.
Route of entry	Inhalation, ingestion or surface skin.
Health effects -	Contact with skin or eyes causes burning and redness. It
common signs and	is a respiratory irritant and can cause shortness of
symptoms	breath, coughing and possible pulmonary oedema.

Substance	**Tar (coal tar)**
Source of exposure	Contact with tar occurs in occupations like asphalting and historically chimney sweeps (soot-tar).
Route of entry	Skin contact.
Health effects - common signs and symptoms	Is known to lead to cancers of the skin (especially of the scrotum) and lung and the causative agents are thought to be polycyclic hydrocarbons. A epidemiological study showed an increased incidence of buccal, colorectal and prostatic cancer, and also leukaemia. Skin tumours (tar warts) are most likely and occur at sites most exposed to the carcinogen. They are sometimes benign but tend to progress to malignant forms and are often multiple affecting the surface (squamous) or underlying (basal cell) tissues of the epidermis. Tar work can also blacken the skin over years.
Substance	**Trichloroethylene (TCE)**
Source of exposure	This is one of the halogenated hydrocarbons widely used in industry because of their non-flammable and non-explosive properties. Highly volatile TCE is used as a metal degreasing agent, for dry-cleaning and as a refrigerant.
Route of entry	The vapour is inhaled and absorbed.
Health effects - common signs and symptoms	TCE liquid and vapour can burn the eyes and skin and corneal ulceration is possible due to its anaesthetic property masking a foreign body in the eye. TCE inhalation is addictive and can also produce kidney and liver damage. Alcohol consumed around the time of exposure causes "degreaser's flush" - bright red face and arms. It is metabolised in the liver and excreted in urine as trichloroacetic acid and trichloroethanol conjugated to glucuronic acid. Its main threat is on acute exposure to high vapour concentration (or rarely ingestion of the liquid). It is a powerful narcotic (it has been used medically as a general anaesthetic) leading to unconsciousness and the danger of death.
Substance	**Vinyl chloride monomer**
Source of exposure	Vinyl chloride monomer (VCM) is used in the manufacture of polyvinyl chloride and workers are most at risk of inhaling VCM vapour when autoclaves used for the polymerisation process are opened and cleaned.
Route of entry	Inhalation
Health effects - common signs and symptoms	The vapour is rapidly absorbed and excreted through the lungs. In acute exposures VCM acts as a narcotic with mild general anaesthetic action.

Chronic low exposure leads to VCM disease, its **metabolism** in the liver leading to antigen formation with an immune response by the body. This response affects many organs but specifically the skin, blood vessels and bones to form the triad of disorders - *scleroderma* (thick, stiff skin leading to clawing of the hands), *Raynaud's phenomenon* (abnormal blanching of the fingers, cold extremities and pins and needles in response to cold conditions) and *acro-osteolysis* (dissolving of bone especially in finger tips and sacroiliac joints). Sufferers of VCM intoxication may also have generalized fatigue and lassitude, together with non-specific abnormalities of liver function reflecting fibrosis or hepatitis-like changes.

A very small proportion of those exposed develop angiosarcoma of the liver, an extremely rare tumour.

Workers can be observed biologically by x-rays of the hands and liver-function tests, with removal from exposure of employees with abnormal findings to avoid liver fibrosis or angiosarcoma. There is no specific treatment for VCM disease. Like asbestos and mesothelioma there is a long latent period between exposure and liver cancer.

Disaster Chronicles

Appendix 3 contains brief outlines intended to highlight the main causes, events, losses, etc, associated with various disasters or notable accidents; for accurate detailed information refer to official reports. They include:

Aberfan
Abbeystead Valve House Explosion
Allied Colloids Fire*
Appleby Frodingham Steelworks Explosion
Associated Octel Fire
Bhopal Toxic Release
Brent Cross Crane Collapse*
Camelford Water Pollution Accident
Chernobyl
Clapham Junction Train Crash*
Flixborough UVCE*
General Foods Explosion
Grangemouth Flare Line Accident*
Grangemouth Explosion*
Herald of Free Enterprise Sinking*
Hickson and Welch Fire*
Kegworth Air Disaster*
Kings Cross Underground Fire
Littlebrook 'D' Hoist Failure*
Markham Colliery Hoist Failure*
Pemex LPG Terminal Explosion, Mexico City*
Piper Alpha Fire*
Piper's Row Car Park Collapse
Port of Ramsgate Walkway Collapse*
Seveso Toxic Release
Three Mile Island Nuclear Accident

* denotes events specifically referenced in the NEBOSH syllabus.

Date   21 October 1966   **Aberfan**

Consequences
At about 9.15 am, thousands of tons of colliery waste swept quickly down the side of Merthyr Mountain, South Wales. It flowed into the village of Aberfan killing 116 children, five teachers and 23 adult inhabitants of Aberfan.

Preconditions
The geology of the underlying environment consists of a series of impervious bands of coal combined with small clay stratum sandwiched by sandstone layers. These bands of coal have the effect of transporting water to the surface and causing localised water logging. This area received very high rainfall throughout the year, and consequently experienced numerous flood periods.

Technical failures
The ability of the coal seams to induce a 'capillary' action, thus drawing the water to the surface caused a complete saturation of a 'slag heap'.

The 'slag heap' consisted of the unconsolidated waste debris as a result of coal mining from the Merthyr Vale Colliery. The mass saturation of tip number 7 caused localised destabilising of the tip this resulted in 140,000 tonnes of the colliery debris flowing from the tip's elevated position

Numerous water pipes were fractured due to the weight of overlying material causing an increase in the water content of the slumping material. This added to the continued flow of material into the village crushing and burying buildings in its path.

Non technical or procedural failures
The tipping gang up the mountain had seen the slide start, but could not raise the alarm because their telephone cable had been repeatedly stolen. (The disaster actually happened so quickly that a telephone warning would not have saved lives).

There was a lack of any regulation on tip safety; siting of the tip was made with little consideration or expert knowledge.

Information from previous occurrences was neglected and inadequately circulated.

Exterior inspections of the slag heap were inadequate a mechanical (not civil) engineer looked after the tips. Local protests over safety were ignored.

Date   23 May 1984   **Abbeystead**

Consequences
Local residents visited because of concern over flooding. Water was pumped in a demonstration this being the first time for 17 days. Before water flowed an explosion ripped the valve house apart killing 8 people. A further 8 people died later. (Total 13 visiting residents and 3 Water Authority employees).

Causes
A void had formed in the tunnel connecting the valve house to the pumping station.

The void arose because a valve was left partly open because of silting problems, regardless of whether pumping or not. (Contrary to design rules).

Geological methane gas built up in the void.

When pumping started the methane gas in the void was pushed to the vent chamber

which then vented to atmosphere through the valve house rather than through a vent stack.
Ignition of the gas may have been by smoking materials or electrical equipment.

Date 21 July 1992   **Allied Colloids Limited Fire**

Consequences
The fire spread throughout the warehouse and smoke was blown towards nearby motorways. The fire was contained that day but the fire brigade was not stood down until 18 days later due to risk of re-ignition during clean up. Considerable environmental damage to the Aire and Calder rivers resulted from the firewater run off. The seat of the fire was located in a raw materials warehouse at Allied Colloids site in Low Moor, Bradford.

Preconditions
The warehouse had two rooms allocated for the storage of oxidising and flammable products known as No.1 and No. 2 oxystores. No. 2 oxystore had steam heating as it was originally designed to store frost sensitive products. On the morning of the incident steam heated blowers in the warehouse had been turned on to dry out moisture. It is thought that a steam condensate line was responsible for heating a number of AZDN kegs, which were stored at height some of which ruptured and spilled white powder over the floor. It was determined that no immediate hazard was present and the AZDN data sheet was referred to before a clean up plan was devised. While waiting for confirmation from the appropriate vacuum cleaner manufacturer an employee noticed a plume of smoke/vapour and a hissing noise coming from a bag of SPS that was located underneath the AZDN kegs. Before the employee could douse the SPS with water the vapour plume ignited and became a jet flame of about 300 mm in length. Within a few seconds the jet flame became a flash fire which was transmitted all around the room.
Technical failures
AZDN kegs were stored in the same section of the warehouse as SPS and other oxidising substances. Poor control over the segregation of hazardous materials.
It was determined later that the AZDN powder probably mixed with unintended spills of SPS and other oxidising products. AZDN in contact with SPS is likely to have been ignited by an impact, possibly from a lid and associated metal ring closure from one of the damaged AZDN kegs falling onto a bag or the floor.
Failure of the steam heating system or operator error meant that heating was applied in No. 2 oxystore as well as in the main warehouse.
The oxystores and warehouse were not fitted with adequate smoke detection and fire fighting facilities. Neither active nor passive fire protection
Non technical or procedural failures
Documentation wrongly classified the powder.
The fire brigade and police should have been informed immediately the first incident had been discovered. There was a 50 minute delay before the fire occurred and the emergency services informed.
Emergency response and spill control was poor and the site emergency plan inadequate.
No secondary containment: bunds, catchpots, barriers existed.

Date 1975   **Appleby Frodingham Steelworks Explosion**

Consequences
Not so much an explosion as an eruption of molten metal which occurred after water ingressed the process by leaking from a cooling system.

Technical failures
Corrosion of a steel blanking plug located in a copper cooler which is directly related to the contact of the two metals widely separated in the electro-chemical series. There was nothing to prevent ingress of water to molten metal.

Non technical or procedural failures
Failure to follow original design drawings (drawings not available).
Lack of knowledge existed of corrosion potential of dissimilar metals.
No planned maintenance schedule existed.
There was a failure to assess the potential for the risks involved with water mixing with molten metal.

Date February 1994   **Associated Octel Fire**

Consequences
In spite of pre-arranged procedures for dealing with major incidents involving chemical release a pool of ethyl chloride collected and the vapours ignited causing a major pool fire which was most intense at the base of the reactor. As the incident developed there were also fires at flanges damaged in the fire, including jet flames at the top of two large process vessels on the plant. No serious injuries, ill health or environmental effects resulted from the release and fire but this was a serious incident at a major hazard site. The plant itself was extensively damaged, requiring a complete rebuild.

Preconditions
In the hours leading up to the release, process data indicating pump P251/3 had stopped appeared to be misinterpreted by process operators. Subsequently plant alarm signals were overlooked. Even if appropriate corrective action had been taken at this stage, the incident would still have occurred (the release occurred when the replacement pump P251/2 was switched on). However, the net result of the operators losing track of the process dynamics was that a much larger inventory of process liquids than normal had built up in the EC plant, mainly in the slops drum. This contributed to the scale and duration of the release and subsequent fire.

Technical failures
The immediate technical cause of the incident was the failure of a pipe work component leading to a major release of process liquids, the underlying reason was a failure to identify the risk of a major release in this part of the EC plant.
The initial release occurred at a point between fixed pipework and the discharge port of a pump recycling ethyl chloride to the reactor, as a result of either (a) a corroded securing flange on the pump working loose or (b) the failure of a PTFE bellows connecting the pump discharge to the pipe.
Only a visual alarm and no audible alarm existed to signify that pump 251/3 had stopped. Even the visual alarm was confusing. There was no record of the type of alarms which should have been provided for this pump.

132

There was evidence that the alarms may have been altered since the new control panel had been installed.

Non technical or procedural failures

Experience of running the plant over the last 22 years and the pattern of breakdown maintenance, albeit not formally recorded, had suggested a risk of minor leaks rather than a single major breach of containment. Undue reliance was placed on this and although a major hazard review was conducted by the company in 1984 this did not place sufficient emphasis on a fundamental assessment of inherent risks in the design of the EC plant.

Moreover, the most significant major hazard on the site as a whole arose from the storage and use of chlorine and the company directed a lot of its attention towards the identification and management of toxic hazards.

As a direct result of the failure to conduct a fundamental assessment of the inherent risk, insufficient attention was paid to a range of safety precautions which would have reduced or avoided the risk of a major release or mitigated its effects.

There was no formal system of routine visual inspection of pipe work, discharge ports, pumps and other components in this part of the EC plant.

Maintenance of these components was on a breakdown basis and no written records of the frequency of component failure or replacement were kept.

Other factors such as the misalignment of a motor drive coupling and misalignment of bolt on the flange were also the consequence of poor installation and maintenance and increased the risk of failure of the pump, its flanges and joints. If an adequate system of planned maintenance had been in place the risk of this incident occurring would have been greatly reduced.

Date   December 1984   **Bhopal**

Consequences

Underground storage tank released a vapour cloud of methyl isocyanate (mic) which killed 2500 people and seriously injured thousands.

Preconditions

Mic stored at 0-15 °C by refrigerant system in stainless steel tanks designed to withstand 40 psig and full vacuum. Precautions included a flare line in case scrubbers failed and an empty tank for emergency transfer of mic. A 'township' of local people had grown up around the site at the boundary walls and fences.

Technical Failures

The refrigerant system was out of service.

The flare line was out of commission for repairs.

The vent scrubber was switched off and of insufficient capacity.

Tank pressure and temperature indicators did not work.

Tank temperature increased.

Non technical or procedural failures

Rapid (unexpected) vaporisation of mic.

Release of mic to local environment.

The local population was not warned of release.

The local population was not instructed in emergency actions.

Spare tank not used for transfer.

Operators and supervisors were inexperienced and poorly trained.

Date 1964   **Brent Cross Crane Collapse**

Consequences

The Brent Cross shopping centre is a landmark at the point at which the London North Circular Road conjoins with the M1 motorway. In 1964 in the early stages of construction the jib of a mobile crane collapsed as it was erecting the king post of a scotch derrick crane. The king post fell onto a passing coach killing 7 and injuring a further 32 passengers.

Preconditions

The crane was set on a slope of 1:30 which caused a small lateral force to be created at the jib head when the load was lifted. A bending moment was created which increased in magnitude along the length of the jib.

Technical Failures

An additional section of jib, a "gate", was fitted which allowed the jib to be folded for transport. The fixing lugs for the gate were not manufactured to drawing specification. The lugs should have been rectangular which would have transmitted compressive forces axially through the assembly instead they were made triangular to match the hinge assembly. Once assembled the forces exerted were transmitted directly through the lug pins increasing the stresses on the jib members by a factor of 10.

The gate was fitted at the heel of the jib instead of at head section. The designer intended the assembly to operate under tension not compression.

The load being lifted was 7 tons 17cwt which exceeded the safe working load of the crane by 5% (SWL 7 tons 10cwt).

SWL indicator on the crane was not operational.

Non technical or procedural failures

Failure to follow design drawings in the manufacture of the fixing lugs and absence of procedures to detect such deviation.

Failure to provide proper assembly instructions regarding positioning of the gate.

Failure to carry out routine statutory inspections of the crane (9 breaches of lifting regulations in total).

Date 6 July 1988   **Camelford Water Pollution Incident**

Consequences

Contaminated water was delivered to around 7000 homes at Camelford. Hundreds of people suffered nausea, vomiting, diarrhoea and other medical problems.

Preconditions

20 tons of aluminium sulphate solution delivered by a chemical company to the wrong tank.

Non technical or procedural failures (mainly)

Aluminium sulphate is normally added in small quantities during water treatment process.

The tank concerned contained 300,000 gallons of purified water destined for domestic consumption.
Vital hours were lost in dealing with the pollution as the standby officer was unavailable. It was 12 hours before any warning was given.

Date   25 April 1986   **Chernobyl**

Consequences
The Chernobyl accident killed more than 30 people immediately and, as a result of the high radiation levels in the surrounding 20-mile radius, 135,00 people had to be evacuated.

Preconditions
The World's worst nuclear power accident occurred at Chernobyl in the former USSR (now Ukraine). The power plant located 80 miles north of Kiev had 4 reactors and whilst testing reactor number 4 a number of safety procedures were disregarded. At 1:23am the chain reaction in the reactor became out of control creating explosions and a fireball which blew off the reactor's heavy steel and concrete lid.

Technical failures
The RBMK reactor type used at Chernobyl suffers from instability at low power and thus may experience a rapid, uncontrollable power increase. Although other reactor types have this problem they incorporate design features to stop instability from occurring.
The cause of this instability is water which acts as a moderator and neutron absorber (slowing down the reaction) whilst steam does not.
Excess steam pockets in the RBMK design lead to an increased power generation known as a positive void coefficient. This in turn causes additional heating producing more steam which means less neutron absorption causing the problem to escalate.
This all happens very rapidly and if it is not stopped quickly it is very hard to stop as it supplies itself.
The sudden increase in temperature caused part of the fuel to rupture, fuel particles then reacted with the water creating a steam explosion which destroyed the reactor core. A second explosion added to the destruction two minutes later.

Non technical or procedural failures
The organisations responsible for the Chernobyl Nuclear Power plant lacked a 'safety culture' resulting in an inability to remedy design weaknesses despite being known about before the accident.
While running a test of the reactor numerous safety procedure were violated by the station technicians.
Only 6 to 8 control rods were used during the test despite the existence of a standard operating order which stated that a minimum of 30 rods were required to retain control.
The reactor's emergency cooling system was disabled.
The test was carried out without a proper exchange of information between the team in charge of the test and personnel responsible for the operation of the nuclear reactor.

Date   12 December 1988   **Clapham Junction**

Consequences
The driver of a commuter train stopped to report it had crossed red signal. The signal did not remain red and a second train crashed into back. A third train travelling in the opposite direction hit the overturned carriages. 35 died and 500 were injured.

Technical Failures
An extra wire made contact with relay in signal box causing faulty signalling. The extra wire should have been cut back and insulated in recent rewiring work carried out as part of major overhaul. This procedure was detailed in instruction SI-16.
Non technical or procedural failures
The technician who did the rewiring did not know of SI-16 and had received little training; his errors were characteristic features of his work (since joining in 1972).
The supervisor did not check his technician's work as required by instruction SL-53 (testing), he did not know of SL-53.
The Area Engineer did not follow or implement SL-53 as he neither knew of it nor thought it his responsibility. SL-53 was issued without instruction, seminars or training. Management did not monitor implementation of SL-53 because they thought it was being done.
Certain managers had been specifically appointed to raise the standard of testing (SL-53) as a result of incidents. They didn't know what was required of them.
The rewiring programme's original planning had been superseded by staff reductions. Overtime working was extensive. The technician had worked for 3 months with only one day off.
Senior management lacked knowledge of and concern for safety issues.
No proper training, job descriptions, communication systems, standards setting, monitoring existed together with poor planning and excessive working hours, led to this disaster.
British Rail's reporting of the event to emergency services was slow.

Date   1 June 1974   **Flixborough**

Consequences
An explosion at Nypro chemical works caprolactum plant killed 28 people on site (18 in control room). There was extensive devastation, widespread injuries and damage to local community. 53 casualties in all and 2000 properties damaged.

Preconditions
The failure of a temporary bypass pipe between pressure reactors 4 and 6 which had been installed to facilitate continued operation of the plant after failures had been identified in no. 5 reactor. Insufficient nitrogen blanketing gas was available during start up of the plant following the bypass installation. Cyclohexane vapour release from the failure formed an unconfined vapour cloud which was ignited from a source on the ground. The large inventory: 330,000 gal cyclohexane; 66,000 gal naphtha; 11,000 gal toluene and 26,000 gal benzene contributed to the proportions of the disaster (licensing only related to 7,000 gall gasoline). It was suggested that a sudden pressure increase

may have arisen from vapour evolution from superheated water layer in reactor 4. This layer may have developed because an agitator was not in use at the time.

Technical failures

Stress corrosion of vessel 5 which was caused by nitrates present in water sprayed onto the reactor.

Rise in internal pressure was greater than that normally expected.

The by-pass pipe (20 inch diameter) was unsuitable and incapable of performing its expected function.

The offset (dogleg) between reactors 4 and 6 caused a high bending moment when the increased pressure passed through.

The supporting framework around the pipe was incapable of restraining the movement generated.

Non technical or procedural failures

The plant had insufficient competent persons (no works engineer, no qualified mechanical engineer). Many staff were overworked.

No procedures existed to control plant or process modifications.

No checks were made on identical reactors for similar corrosion.

The linking pipe was badly designed with no reference to available standards or manufacturer's guidelines which would have shown that is was unsuitable. Bypass engineering design was of a poor technical standard and introduced a weakness into pipe work connecting pressure vessels.

Production pressures were applied to engineers to complete the task quickly.

No proof tests were made or inspections of the assembly carried out.

No investigation of the failure of reactor 5 was carried out prior to restarting the process.

Date   6 July 1988   **Piper Alpha**

Consequences

A series of explosions and fire on the Occidental platform Piper Alpha resulted in 167 deaths.

Preconditions

A flammable gas build up resulting from leak from condensate injection pump ignited. The pump had been shut down (day shift) to remove a safety pressure valve for recertification, a blind flange assembly fitted in its place. On the nightshift a second pump failed and the first pump was restarted. Condensate entered the relief line and gas escaped from the non-airtight flange assembly. The initial blast put out main power supplies and emergency systems failed.

How the system should have worked

Maintenance work needed signature of approval authority (AA).

Designated Authority (DA) then lists safety precautions.

DA signs to confirm isolation.

Performing Authority (PA) required to comply with conditions.

If work completed during shift PA signs to indicate.

Permit returned to DA.

DA to inspect equipment and confirm safe/not safe to restart.

If not safe to restart or work not completed permit sent to DA stating this.

DA signs to acknowledge suspension of maintenance/not safe to restart.

Suspended permit displayed in control room - equipment to remain isolated.

Non technical or procedural failures

No valve locking-off procedure was included in permit.

Suspended permits were not displayed in control room.

Work on the pump was suspended without inspection by Designated Authority; a frequent practice.

Multiple jobs were listed on one permit.

Failure to display permit at worksite.

Inaccurate description of work.

Permit system monitored daily, audited frequently. Failures not identified.

A similar permit failure in 1987 resulted in a fatal accident (no permit issued - prosecution under HSW s3). No changes made since.

Designated Authorities not trained.

Inaccurate information given in safety handbook.

Evacuation drills not frequently carried out.

Training in procedures poor.

Date 13 March 1987   **Grangemouth (1)**

Consequences

The release of flammable liquid from a flare line pipe ignited resulting in two fatalities.

Preconditions

A valve removal from flare line pipe required work to be controlled by permit. Access was by scaffold tower and a crane was provided to support the valve and remove it.

A mobile air compressor supplied air line breathing apparatus and a water curtain set up to prevent escaping gases being ignited by adjacent plant. The flare line pipe contained large inventory of liquid.

Technical failures

Isolation valves, although closed as tightly as possible, were not fully closed. This was clearly observable.

Only one test of line drainage carried out (by opening a drain line).

Warning of liquid content (leaking during bolt removal) not considered important or thoroughly checked by supervisor.

Exhaust spark arrestor missing from compressor.

Non technical or procedural failures

Emergency escape from scaffold was inadequate.

Decisions about procedures and safety precautions which should have been made at senior level were left to supervisors.

Verification of flare line pipe drainage relied on opening one small bore drain line only. These were known to be prone to blockage at least two should have been checked.

Warning indications were ignored. Steam or nitrogen should have been used to verify drain lines clear before reliance on this as a test of flare line pipe drainage.

The procedure for removing valve was inadequate.

Ignition prevention measures and provision of means of escape from scaffold were inadequate.

Internal code requiring open/closed indicators on valves was ignored.

Date 22 March 1987   **Grangemouth (2)**

Consequences

Explosion and fire at BP Grangemouth resulting in one fatality. The explosion of a pressure vessel created extensive blast damage and a fireball. (Site was controlled by CIMAH Regs).

Preconditions

High pressure (HP) and Low pressure (LP) vessels were used to separate light gases from liquid. Liquids passed from the HP separator to the LP separator via a pipe work system at the base of the HP vessel. The liquid level in the HP vessel prevented gas pressure being transmitted to the LP vessel which was not designed to take high pressure. Because of modifications, removal of trip systems, operator errors and mistakes over the status of valves the HP vessel emptied its liquid content into the LP vessel allowing gas to pressurise the LP vessel beyond its design capability. The LP relief valve could not cope and explosive failure occurred.

Technical failures

Disconnections and modifications to trip systems were made (because of faults, process difficulties and false alarms) without consideration of the consequences.
The low pressure vessel had insufficient relief capacity for the foreseeable event.

Non technical or procedural failures

Too much reliance was placed on operators for the safe operation of plant.
Operators had insufficient appreciation of the risks involved.
Procedures for testing interlocks and trips were inadequate and, in any case, ignored.
Action points from audits, which had revealed the faults and the potential for gas breakthrough, were never carried out.

Date 18 November 1981   **General Foods: Banbury**

Consequences

Process plant failure led to the emission of corn starch powder (custard process) which ignited and exploded. 9 employees were injured and extensive building damage resulted. (Primary explosion only. Overpressure estimate - 7-16 kN/m^2).

Preconditions

Starch powder (2 tons) was pneumatically fed to a process feed bin (capacity 3 tons) from a central hopper. The hopper served 3 feed bins via a diverter valve. This was centrally controlled by a control room operator when requested by the production line. After filling feed bin 1 the control room operator switched the diverter valve to bin 2. This was confirmed by control panel display. A further 2 tons of powder was transferred.

Technical failures

The diverter valve had not moved because of a blockage and 2 tons of powder went to bin 1 (already filled).
Air + powder pressure caused sides of feed bin to bulge and parts of unit to fail.
There were no safety devices to prevent overfilling of feed bins (nor any low level indicators).
A dust cloud was generated by continued powder feed which was further dispersed by

the compressed air supply to a filter unit which had become detached.

Ignition was provided by electrical arcing when the electrical supply to unit ruptured due to the distortion of the feed bin.

No explosion relief was provided.

Non technical or procedural failures

In spite of its known explosion potential necessary precautions were not taken.

There was inadequate maintenance of diverter valve even though evidence indicated the need for regular maintenance (high position made access difficult).

Inadequate design of system:

The control panel display was activated by the diverter valve control switch not the actual position of the valve.

No indication of starch levels in the bins was provided, the panel indicators simply confirmed transfer of 2 tons of powder.

Feed bins were not designed for pressure nor were pressure relief valves fitted.

Feed bins were not visible to the control room operator.

Date 6th March 1987   **Herald Of Free Enterprise**

Consequences

On leaving Zeebrugge, the Herald capsized to port and settled on sandbanks mostly below water. 192 deaths.

Preconditions

The Herald set sail with both inner and outer bow doors open. As it increased speed it took on water which flooded G deck causing it to capsize.

Technical failures

Berth loading ramp designed for single deck ferries meant Herald had to trim the ship nose down by filling ballast tanks. This allowed loading of upper car deck.

Most lifejackets locked away to stop vandalism.

Shortage of rope ladders.

Emergency lighting on board was poor.

Sailings with doors open had happened previously. [Once deliberately (doors jammed open) in calm seas with a look-out monitoring the bow wave].

Non technical or procedural failures

The Chief Officer (loading officer duty) was to ensure the doors were closed before sailing but was also required to be on the bridge 15 minutes before sailing.

The Assistant Boatswain's duty was to close the doors but he was asleep in his cabin after relief from maintenance and cleaning duties.

The Boatswain noticed doors open but did not close them; it was not his duty.

No orders existed (system of work) requiring positive statement of door closure to bridge ("Doors Closed" could not be visually confirmed from bridge).

The Captain assumed doors to be closed unless told to contrary.

There was great pressure to sail on time or even early. Late sailings were not acceptable to the company who placed considerable pressure to achieve fast turn around times.

Repeated requests for bow door indicators on bridge were never answered; requests were treated negatively. (Cost about £500).

Herald (Roll on - Roll off) design was inherently unsafe - top heavy.

Consequences

At approximately 13:20 hrs whilst cleaning sludge from the vessel an incandescent conical jet erupted from the access hole. This projected horizontally towards the 'Meissner' control building. A vertical jet of burning vapours shot out of the top rear vent to the height of the distillation column nearby. The jet fire lasted for approximately one minute before subsiding to localised fires around the buildings nearby. The force of the jet destroyed the scaffold, in the process, propelling the access cover into the centre of the Meissner control building. The jet severely damaged this building and then impacted on the north face of the main office block causing a number of fires to start inside the building. A total of 22 fire appliances and over 100 fire fighters attended the incident.

Preconditions

A clean out operation of a batch still, known as '60 still base', was organised in order to remove residues. This vessel had never been cleaned since it was installed in 1961. An operator dipped the sludge to examine it and reported the sludge as gritty with the consistency of soft butter to management. In order to soften the sludge, which was estimated to have a depth of 34 cm, steam was applied to the bottom battery. Advice was given not to exceed 90°C. Employees started the clean out operation using a metal rake. The material was tar-like and had liquid entrained in it. Approximately one hour into the cleaning process a longer rake was used to reach further into the still. When the vessel's temperature gauge in the control room was reported to be reading 48°C, instructions were given to isolate the steam.

Technical failures

A faulty pressure reducing valve on steam supply supplied steam at a higher temperature than anticipated.

The still base inlet was not isolated prior to the work commencing.

A metal rake was used to clean the sludge from the still containing flammable vapours.

Maintenance procedures did not require flame/spark proof tools.

Non technical or procedural failures

The decision to clean out the vessel for the first time after 30 years of operation fell outside routine maintenance procedures and systems.

Two permits were issued for the removal of the access cover and one permit for the blanking of the still base inlet. No permit to work was ever issued for the task of raking out the still base.

Failure to analyse the sludge and atmosphere within the vessel prior to cleaning. No sample was sent for analysis nor was the atmosphere inside the vessel checked for a flammable vapour. It was mistakenly thought that the material was a thermally stable tar.

Inadequate measurement of sludge temperature was due to the position of the temperature probe.

No classification of the hazardous area meant no flame proofing or identification and elimination of ignition sources.

Poor plant layout put occupied buildings near high hazard plant which produced casualties from within control room and administration block.

Date 23 May 1984   **Kegworth Air Disaster**

Consequences

A BMA Boeing 737 crashed on the western embankment of the M1 motorway. Having obtained clearance for an emergency landing at East Midlands Airport, the malfunctioning engine suffered a major loss of thrust when power had been increased to it on the final approach. Thirty nine passengers died in the accident and a further eight passengers died later from their injuries. Of the remaining seventy nine passengers seventy four suffered serious injury.

Preconditions

While climbing to cruising altitude the aircraft began to shake and the flight deck filled with smoke, instruments indicated an engine failure. When asked by the captain which engine had failed, the first officer replied: *"it's the le...it's the right one"* when in fact, it was the left engine that had failed. An incorrect conclusion was drawn by the flight crew as to the identity of a malfunctioning engine. Subsequently the wrong engine was shut down. Passengers and three of the cabin staff had witnessed sparks and smoke coming out of the left engine through the port windows. To allay concerns the captain broadcast to the passengers that there was trouble with the *right* engine and that the flight was being diverted to EM airport. Although the passengers were confused by the discrepancy no one brought this to the attention of the cabin staff.

Technical failures

The engine instrument display layout was severely criticised by the Air Accident Investigation Branch in that it was open to confusion, i.e. left and right engine information could be mixed.

Vibration indicators were smaller and less conspicuous in new 737 compared with previous layouts.

Non technical or procedural failures

The captain ordered shut down the right engine (which was still serviceable) shortly after which the smoke and fume in the cabin abated. This confirmed to the captain that he had made the correct decision despite the fact that the vibration indicator on the left engine remained at maximum.

The flight attendants claimed (later) that they had not heard the captain's reference to the *right* engine.

This aircraft was a new 737; conversion training for flight crew was poor/short and involved no simulation.

Instrumentation in previous versions of the 737 was very similar. With lack of training on new version, old habits and expectations may have dominated decisions and actions.

Cabin staff/flight crew do not train in emergency procedures together.

The Captain's previous experience of many flight hours in DC 9 aircraft associated with unreliable vibration indication instruments, added to his perception that such instruments were not dependable.

First officer's mistaken identification was made under considerable stress causing him to possibly fall back on 'perceptual set'.

No convention existed as to engine identification terminology. The left engine may also be referred to as No. 1 or port engine while the right engine may be referred to as No.2 or starboard engine.

Date   18 Nov 1987   **Kings Cross**

Consequences
Fire at Kings Cross Underground. 31 people killed.

Preconditions
A discarded cigarette end ignited grease and rubbish in the running track of wooden escalator no. 4.   A passenger alerted the booking clerk who phoned the relief station inspector (RSI).   Evacuation of passengers was initiated by railway police.   RSI inspected the lower machine room and found no fire. The RSI then inspected the upper machine room; found a fire but did not activate water fog system.   Trains were under orders not to stop but continued to do so.

Technical failures
The running tracks of the escalator were not regularly cleaned; dust and grease was allowed to build up on the tracks. There was some confusion over maintenance cleaning responsibility.
A recommendation to replace wooden escalators with metal ones following a previous underground fire was never implemented.

Non technical or procedural failures
Training of staff in evacuation and fire drills was inadequate.
No evacuation plan existed for underground.
RSI not trained.
RSI did not inform station manager nor line controller (trains continued to stop).
Locked doors and metal barriers impeded escape.
Many CCTV monitors were inoperative or switched off.
'Smoulderings' (fires) regarded as inevitable - consequence of old plant. There were many such events which were of little consequence and staff became complacent.
Railway inspectorate did not pursue fire issues.

Date   9 Jan 1978   **Littlebrook 'D' Power Station Hoist Failure**

Consequences
The single rope of a hoist cage broke killing four and seriously injuring another five men. As the cage fell through 30 metres to the bottom of the 60 metre shaft the safety gear failed to restrain it.

Technical failures
The suspension rope failed at a point weakened by corrosion and devoid of lubricant. 35 metres of rope was found to be in this condition.
Many individual wires in the rope were broken and of those remaining their tensile strength was reduced to between 50% and 80% of their original strength.
Corrosion occurred in a very short period and was consistent with the likely impregnation of salt water. This was in evidence in the shaft.
The clamping units of the cages fall-arrest mechanism were corroded and were deposited with cement-like scale.

Non-technical or procedural failures
The statutory six-monthly inspection was overdue.
Defects were not observed on the weekly site inspection.

No maintenance records were kept.

The hoist owner's policy failed to specify detailed procedures to meet its objectives.

The site agent was responsible for plant maintenance and records but had no training or guidance to carry out this work.

Date 30 July 1973   **The Markham Colliery Accident**

Consequences

A winding engine raising and lowering cages in a mineshaft failed to stop; the descending cage struck the bottom of the shaft while the ascending cage struck the mine headgear. Eighteen miners riding in the descending cage were killed, eleven were injured and the winding engine driver was injured as debris was pulled into the winding engine house. This kind of accident is known as "over winding", and was the most feared of the types of accidents which could occur with winding of cages in mine shafts.

Preconditions

The brakes on this winding engine consisted of large shoes pressed upwards on to tracks on either side of the winding drum. They were held "off" by compressed air in a brake cylinder, which operated against a nest of springs. When the brake was applied, air was released from the cylinder, and the nest of springs forced the brake shoes against the drum. If the brake cylinder or air supply failed, then the springs should force the brakes "on".

Technical failures

The steel rod through the centre of the spring nest had broken through fatigue, so the spring nest was ineffective; there was no spring compression with which the brakes could be applied. Failure of the rod accounts for the total loss of braking.

The operation of the emergency stop button cut off all power to the system which eliminated the ability to use regenerative braking which would have lessened the severity of the impact.

When the operator tried to trip the "ungabbing" gear, this, too, depended on the brake mechanism being capable of being applied by the pressure of the spring nest. With the rod broken, the spring pressure was no longer there.

The rod was a "single line" component. In other words, if it failed, then the braking system as a whole failed. Many parts of the brake system were duplicated, eg shoes, tracks, but there was only one spring nest rod, and if it failed, then it failed to danger.

A similar failure of a spring nest rod had occurred at Ollerton Colliery in 1961, when stresses induced by bending were the cause of failure. As a result, the NCB had issued an instruction that all spring nest rods were to be examined, but not how often, nor was there any mention of non-destructive testing.

Non technical or procedural failures

The spring nest rod at Markham had been visually examined shortly after that instruction, but not tested, and there was no provision for non-destructive testing or a scheme of examination at Markham.

It was shown that, although the cracks in the spring nest rod would not have been readily detected visually or by ultrasonic testing, they could have been found by magnetic particle detection.

Weaknesses in maintenance were generally observed and whilst many had no bearing on the accident there was evidence of failures to comply with National Coal Board recommendations.

Date 19 Nov 1984   **Pemex LPG Terminal - Mexico City**

Consequences
A major fire and a series of catastrophic explosions occurred and as a consequence of these events some 500 individuals were killed and the terminal destroyed. About fifteen minutes after the initial release the first BLEVE occurred. For the next hour and a half there followed a series of BLEVEs as the LPG vessels violently exploded. LPG was said to rain down and surfaces covered in the liquid were set alight. The explosions which totally destroyed the site were recorded on a seismograph at the University of Mexico.

Preconditions
Three refineries supplied the facility with LPG on a daily basis. The plant was being filled from a refinery 400 km away because, on the previous day, it had become almost empty. Two large spheres and 48 cylindrical vessels were filled to 90% and 4 smaller spheres to 50% full. A drop in pressure was noticed in the control room and also at a pipeline pumping station. An 8-inch pipe between a sphere and a series of cylinders had ruptured but the operators could not identify the cause of the pressure drop. The release of LPG continued for about 5-10 minutes when the gas cloud, estimated at 200 m x 150 m x 2 m high, drifted to a flare stack and ignited causing violent ground shock. A number of ground fires occurred and workers on the plant tried to deal with the escape by various means. At a late stage someone pressed the emergency shut down button.

Technical failures
The installation of a more effective gas detection and emergency isolation system could have averted the incident. The plant had no gas detection system and therefore when the emergency isolation was initiated it was probably too late.
There was a failure of the overall basis of safety which included the layout of the plant (positioning of the vessels) and emergency isolation features.
The terminal's fire water system was disabled in the initial blast and the water spray systems were inadequate.

Non technical or procedural failures
Failure to take account of the survivability of critical systems.
Traffic chaos hindered the arrival of the emergency services which built up as local residents sought to escape the area.
Emergency response was poor; the site emergency plan was inadequate and there was limited access for emergency vehicles.

Date 20 March 1997   **Piper's Row Car Park Collapse, Wolverhampton**

Consequences
A 120 tonne section of the top deck at the Pipers Row multi storey car park collapsed. Although open, the car park was unoccupied and no-one was injured.

Preconditions

Piper's Row car park was a flat slab structure, designed and built in 1964/65 using a technique called 'Lift Slab'. If properly maintained the structure should have had a reasonable margin of strength in relation to the actual loads imposed in use but deterioration of the concrete over and around the column/slab zone led to shear failure of the concrete slab.

Technical failures

The concrete deterioration resulted from localised breakdown of the overlying waterproofing membrane.

Water ingress to areas of poor quality concrete in the upper part of the slab lead to frost damage and a loss of strength.

Assessment of structural integrity of this form of 'Lift Slab' structure requires cautious engineering judgement otherwise an under estimation of load acting on the structure, and an over estimation of strength can result.

Reinforced concrete structures of this type may risk progressive collapse following punching shear failure unless adequate bottom reinforcement over the columns is provided.

Non technical or procedural failures

Concerns existed about the generalised robustness requirements in available design codes.

Inspection procedures in place were not sufficiently robust.

Date   23 May 1984   **Port of Ramsgate Walkway Collapse**

Consequences

A passenger walkway bridge from the dock to the ship collapsed killing six and injuring seven others.

Technical failures

No allowance was made in design for 'roll'.

Temporary measures taken to correct a shortfall in the length of the walkway damaged an edge beam.

Some greasomatics were left out of the final assembly.

Bearings and welds suffered metal fatigue.

A final torsional twist of the walkway led to its final collapse.

Non technical or procedural failures

The designer was inexperienced in this type of structure.

There was a possible misconception about the design of the bearings which were assumed to accommodate torsion.

Exterior inspections were inadequate and did not disclose problems.

Date   10 July 1976   **Seveso**

Consequences
Safety valve vented TCDD* (about 2kg) which drifted and was brought down by rain over Seveso (15 miles from Milan). (TCDD is extremely toxic with carcinogenic properties absorbed via inhalation, ingestion or skin routes leading to chloracne, skin burns, rashes, liver/kidney damage, CNS damage, death).   *TCDD 2,3,7,8 (Tetra chloro dibenzo para dioxin) - an undesired by-product. Insoluble in water. By August it was discovered that contamination was more extensive - about 7km x 3km to a 5 microgram/square metre level).

Preconditions
Because it is insoluble in water rain will not disperse. Burning it requires 1000°C which is difficult to achieve. It can be dissolved in olive oil to allow UV breakdown but rain would wash contaminated oil to water table. Similar previous accidents with TCDD proved decontamination to be unsuccessful; with much smaller releases (0.2kg) factories had been dismantled and buried in concrete.

Technical failures
The reactor had gone out of control.
Overheating of its contents caused a safety valve to open.
The high temperature favoured abnormal quantity of TCDD production.
The safety valve did not vent to an enclosed system safety.

Non technical or procedural failures
Local authorities could not be contacted because it was a holiday weekend so little immediate action taken.
Authorities found it difficult to establish from the company, the details of the release and the measures to take.
On day 5, after animal deaths and human illnesses local people were warned not to touch vegetation.
Roads through area remained open.
17 days later a limited evacuation was ordered after 250 cases of poisoning.

Date   28 March 1979   **Three Mile Island Nuclear Incident**

Consequences
Nuclear reactor core damage and radioactive water loss (to containment) in Harrisburg, Pensylvania.

Technical failures
Maintenance workers introduced water into the instrument air system which caused the turbine to trip and feedwater pumps to stop.
Emergency pumps started but their flow was blocked by closed valves which had not been reset on completion of previous maintenance.
The closed valve warning light was hidden by maintenance tags.
The core temperature rose and the reactor tripped opening pressure relief valves (PRV).
The PRV stuck open.

Non technical or procedural failures
The indicator light indicated PRV open and was closed. The light went out but the PRV stayed open. The light was controlled by switch not PRV.
Radioactive water was discharged to containment from PRV.
Diagnosis of water loss from PRV was not made for 2 hours; this water loss caused damage to the reactor.
The control panel was poorly designed. Hundreds of alarms were illogically arranged with no means of isolating unimportant ones. Controls went off scale and key indicators were sited out of view.
Training to handle emergencies was poor.
Previous failures of "PRV stuck open" were neither communicated nor acted upon.